RAISIN BRAN AND OTHER

*30 Years of Lobbying for the most
Famous Tiger in the World*

Cereal

WARS

GEORGE FRANKLIN

RAISIN BRAN AND OTHER CEREAL WARS
30 YEARS OF LOBBYING FOR THE
MOST FAMOUS TIGER IN THE WORLD

iUniverse books may be ordered through booksellers or by contacting:

iUniverse LLC
1663 Liberty Drive
Bloomington, IN 47403
www.iuniverse.com
1-800-Authors (1-800-288-4677)

ISBN: 978-1-4917-3919-8 (sc)
ISBN: 978-1-4917-3920-4 (e)

Printed in the United States of America.

iUniverse rev. date: 08/08/2014

Acknowledgements

My mission with this book was to write, in non-textbook fashion, an overview of the corporate government relations function for those in business or school needing or desirous of a familiarity with what it entails.

The task seemed daunting as I began to put pen to paper until I realized other people had already written it for me.

There was Congressman Frank "Thompy" Thompson from New Jersey who needed a go-for and said he would fire me unless I went back to college and finished law school. His Counsel, Hugh Duffy, who got me the job through "reverse affirmative action" and became a mentor. Judy Simmons, Thompy's personal secretary and gatekeeper, who always kept the gate open for me and who I will always remember fondly. Faye Padgett, constituent caseworker, who covered for me when I was nowhere to be found, and Billy Deitz, the Administrative Assistant, who kept the trains running on time and the press at bay.

After leaving Thompy's office the next chapters were written by Gary Frink who broke me in to the lobby business by showing me how lawyer/lobbyists dress, think and act. Tom Jolly who taught a lot of people, myself included, about loyalty in a town where it is often fleeting, and Earl Leonard of Coca-Cola, who unknowingly gave me my first lessons in corporate government relations.

Kellogg Company wrote the brunt of the book starting when Bill LaMothe, Gary Costley and Peggy Wollerman (now Furth) took a flyer by hiring a 29-year-old relatively inexperienced Washington lawyer/lobbyist to become Director of Government Relations and open a Washington, D.C. office. Scott Campbell, the workaholic General Counsel, showed me how hard it was for "real lawyers" to relate to government relations and how it functions. Joe Stewart, my boss, who hung in there with me despite my being what he termed "an administrative nightmare." Adding to the mix was Rob Crabb, Director of State Taxes, who was/is a steady tell-it-like-it-is-kind of guy and who only rarely tired of me asking "How much is it worth?" before the numbers were in. Also Cliff Gibbons, an outside counsel, who was always organized and tenacious. Finally, Carlos Gutierrez, with whom I shared some fascinating insights and experiences when he became Secretary of Commerce and who never left me hanging when my role with him didn't work out, as well as his administrative assistant Rosemary Johnson who embodies dedication, commitment and hard work.

I want to thank all of these people for writing this book.

Thanks are not enough to the indefatigable Becky O'Dell, who kept the whole publishing process on track and Dick Lovell who gave me his "red pen treatment" as a final safeguard against grammatical and spelling errors. I also want to thank my daughter Katy for her perseverance, organization, criticisms and overall cheerleading as we put this together and my other daughter Christy, who waded in with the final edit, as well as my very Republican wife Molly, who had to listen to all of this the past year while admonishing me when I cited *The New York Times* that it was simply the Democrat newsletter.

"What is past is prologue."
Inscription on the statue in front of the National Archives building, Washington, D.C.

Introduction

In my thirty-some years of lobbying for Kellogg Company in Washington, D.C., state capitols and around the world, I was repeatedly asked three questions: "How does someone become a lobbyist?," "Why does Kellogg need a lobbyist?," and, more generally, "What do lobbyists do?" It also became apparent how little business people know about government relations, an area of endeavor hardly mentioned, much less taught, in business school. In this narrative I try to answer the three questions and give a feel for the government relations function by describing my experiences, which run the gamut from my duties as an intern on Capitol Hill, representing Kellogg as a lawyer, succeeding Kellogg's lobbyist after he was forced into the Witness Protection Program, and taking on the Federal Trade Commission, the Department of Agriculture, Consumer Groups, and non-governmental organizations (NGOs). I was also heavily involved in the U.S. corporate effort against apartheid, the aftermath of 9/11 and some of the most politically volatile issues of the day. I have met seven Presidents, hundreds of Congressmen, Senators, State Legislators, Ambassadors and other worldwide leaders, while almost being appointed Assistant to Secretary of Commerce Carlos Gutierrez under President George W. Bush. Suffice it to say, lobby life is rich with experiences and a cast of characters that include scoundrels, scallywags, charlatans and, simultaneously, a myriad of classy and dedicated people both in and out of government. All of the aforementioned people and attendant experiences hopefully will give the reader a feel for the world of lobbying for a true American corporate icon, and one of the most famous tigers in the world.

"My advice would be to stay away."
Gordon Strahan, former Nixon aide and indicted Watergate participant when asked for advice for young people coming to Washington, D.C.

"May the future bring all the best to you, your family and friends, and may your mother never find out where you work."
Representative William Hungate, (D) Missouri, addressing his colleagues as he left Congress.

Chapter 1

When flying into Washington, D.C., for business, to work in politics or simply as a tourist, the first thing a passenger may notice is that the plane's approach into Reagan National Airport is quite unusual. On a normal approach to landing, the pilot flies downwind, makes a ninety-degree turn to base and then another ninety-degree turn to final. Typically, downwind, base and final are all straight lines. This is not the case when landing in D.C., where pilots use the river visual approach to Runway 19, which involves following the natural, winding path of the Potomac River. This non-traditional approach is illustrative of where the passenger is going: a place where unusual twists and turns are normal, a place with separate rules from the rest of the country, and a city with a culture and ethos unlike any other. D.C. is where Congress appropriates over four billion dollars a year just to run itself, and the U.S. business community spends over three billion dollars in hopes of having the lobbyists "run" Congress. It is a place where the little-known House Administration Committee can leverage power by controlling parking spaces, and where the table the lobbyist or politician secures at the "in" restaurant is a sign of status. This power and the perception of power, however, are often vicarious and fleeting, given the vicissitudes of elections. D.C. is constantly changing, but it is never really fundamentally different.

Who are these people in power and how did they get to become leaders in the most important and influential country in the world? It all starts with interns. Interns grow up to be Congressmen, Senators, lawyers and lobbyists. People like Mitch McConnell, Paul Ryan and Dick Durbin once were lowly interns, running errands and doing all the grunt work beneath the support staff. Earl Leonard who was one of the top officers of Coca-Cola in charge of government relations, understood that principle from the get go. When he would fly in from Atlanta, he often took interns out to dinner or lunch which always perplexed me as a young lawyer because he could have taken that time to go to dinner with Georgia Senators or Congressmen. Finally one day I asked him, "Why do you take out interns and not more important people like Senators?" to which he replied, "Interns grow up to be Senators."

I was always fascinated by politics. Growing up on the South Side of Chicago where I was friends with Jimmy Ryan, nephew of the famed Dan Ryan, Chair of the Cook County Commission for whom Interstate 90/94 is named, I saw firsthand that a Democrat could plan his victory party the same day he announced his run for office. I also witnessed a system where, if you sought a bid to pave your driveway each bid contained a "fee" that went to the Alderman. In our case that was Alderman Fitzpatrick, my buddy Pete's father. It also was an area in which the Irish, and thereby practically by definition Catholic, juvenile justice system was very different from the surrounding black neighborhoods. Elected officials had power and because they had power, they were held accountable which made it all work.

Garbage was picked up, streets were paved and plowed, and street lights worked. It was all very tidy if the elected officials were Democrats and part of the Daley Machine. Political parlance for the political/patronage system put in place by the late Mayor Richard J. Daley assuring Democratic control of Chicago (most famously known, depending on your politics, for either delivering Chicago and hence Illinois for John F. Kennedy in the 1960 presidential race or in the alternative stealing it from Richard Nixon). Elections had an impact on everyday people and their everyday lives.

After moving to Florida to attend high school, I spent one year at the University of Florida where I did not exactly excel academically. I knew my time at Florida was leading nowhere so I decided to leave and headed to D.C., where I could pursue my lifelong interest in politics. My older sister, Joanne, was living there at the time, and she graciously suggested I come and stay with her while I looked for work. In December of 1970, I set off to find a job in the political arena. I tried first with Congressman Sam Gibbons, (D) Tampa, who would later become famous as the impetus for Tom Brokaw's book "The Greatest Generation." I was unsuccessful in securing a position in his office, because all of his intern slots were filled, but I knew that something would become available on the Hill (as Capitol Hill is commonly referred to). And nowhere but the Hill would do.

Finally, there was an opening with Frank Thompson (aka "Thompy"), a Democrat Congressman from New Jersey. One of his top aides was Hugh Duffy, a politically savvy Irishman from South Boston. Thompy had shared with Hugh Duffy his desire to have a black kid from the District act as his driver and all-around "go-for." Duffy responded sarcastically, "Oh, that's going to look really great having a black kid drive you around." Thompy said, "Well, why don't you go find me a white one, then?" Enter George Franklin as a beneficiary of reverse affirmative action. My attempt to secure this job, however, couldn't have come at a worse time. In January of 1970, there was a leadership struggle in the Democratic Caucus and the leading liberals, Mo Udall of Arizona, John Brademas of Indiana, Phil Burton of California and Tip O'Neill of Massachusetts, were all vying for power. Suffice it to say, Frank Thompson was extremely pre-occupied and because I would be responsible for driving his car, running errands and anything else he could think of, it wasn't practical for me to be hired without meeting him. So for five days, I came to his office on the Hill and waited for five to six hours. I would sit in the lobby of Thompy's office, stare at the walls or read a newspaper or book. Sometimes I would go down to the cafeteria for a coffee or food, but it seemed almost impossible to secure a twenty-minute interview with Thompy which was essential to me being hired. But I stayed and I didn't mind. I wasn't leaving until I got to meet the Congressman. I wasn't giving up. I needed this job, and more importantly, I desperately wanted it. In the end, I waited thirty hours over five days to meet the man, and I would have waited another five days and thirty hours more. At the end of day five, I was finally called in and hired on the spot. I was to be Thompy's "go-for" and I would be paid $250 per month.

On Capitol Hill in 1970, there were just three office buildings for the House of Representatives: the Rayburn, Longworth and Cannon buildings, all named for former Speakers of the House. The Rayburn was the largest, and as the newest and most modern building of them all, it was where Thompy and most of the senior members worked. I was to operate from Room B-346 of the Rayburn Building which housed the offices of the Special Subcommittees on Labor, of which Thompy was chair. The B floor was the ground floor, and I, being 19 years old, found that very fortuitous in my quest to check out the young, female interns who would congregate in the courtyard around the large fountain, especially in the summer months. The Rayburn building was named after Speaker Sam Rayburn, (D) Texas, who was arguably one of the most powerful speakers ever. A famous story about Sam Rayburn recounts when a young boy from his District in Texas wrote him a letter, asking Rayburn if he could please send him a copy of the Rules of the House of Representatives. Rayburn sent the kid his picture.

Soon I was on the payroll darting about the Capitol complex on errands for all of the eighteen staffers almost all of whom had a nickname. There is something about politicians and nicknames. Billy Dietz, Thompy's administrative assistant (now called a chief of staff) was the "Kraut" because of his German heritage. Thompy's secretary was Judy "Whispers" Simmons because she spoke with a low and soft voice. Faye Padgett the case worker was "Big Red," as she was tall with red hair. Hugh Duffy was "Duffer," Dan Kaniewski was "Zonker," and Dan Pollitt was "Professor." They were all my bosses. My nickname came to be "Flash," because of my penchant for getting things done quickly. Thompy actually had two nicknames. In addition to "Thompy," President Kennedy and his confidants called him "Topper," because they claimed he could always top any story or joke. No staff member, fellow Congressman or anyone who ever knew him well ever called him "Frank" or "Mr. Thompson." It was always Thompy or Topper. He was a hard-drinking, chain-smoking raconteur, a U.S. Navy World War II veteran and there was a lot of living in that guy. With looks straight out of central casting for The Congressman, he was a dedicated liberal. He was irreverent, with the language of a sailor, but also had an urbaneness that enabled him to work both the blue collar bars of Trenton and the parlors of Princeton.

As an intern, I had many jobs, one of which was picking up the members of Congress when they were summoned to vote. When that time came, a series of lights lit up on clocks throughout the House Office Buildings, and a series of buzzers would sound. That would be the signal to all of the members of Congress that they were needed to vote on the issue at hand. Back then, a lot of the members of Congress, including Thompy, would go to have lunch at The Democratic Club and usually those lunches would involve a few martinis or "pops." When the lights lit up and the buzzer would sound, my responsibility would be to jump into Thompy's car, which would be parked underneath the Rayburn building, drive to The Democratic Club, collect four or five often feeling-no-pain Congressmen who had gathered there for lunch and drive them back to the Capitol to vote. The Club was a block and a half from the Capitol, but the Congressmen figured why walk when the "kid" (me) could pick them up. Thompy's car was an old Pontiac, and it had what was then called the Seatbelt Interlock System, which meant that if the driver or passenger did not buckle his or her seatbelt, a buzzer would sound until the seatbelt was fastened. One afternoon as Thompy and some of his colleagues climbed into the car to be taken back to the Hill to vote on the current issue, one Congressman began struggling with his seatbelt after one too many "pops." The buzzer was buzzing insistently, annoying everyone. The half-lit Congressman said, "What the hell is that?" to which one of the men in the back replied, "That's the seatbelt interlock system, it doesn't stop buzzing unless you fasten your goddamn seatbelt!" The Congressman in the passenger seat exclaimed, "Did we vote for this shit?" No wonder why Congress is held in such disdain!

Another of my responsibilities was distributing mail and making sure the bucket of ice, which was left in front of the office every morning, made it back to what we called the "trophy cabinet", aka bar. To accomplish this, I'd arrive at 8 a.m., sort through the mail, which would be tied up in string, and distribute it to everyone in the office. Come mid-morning, around ten or ten thirty, Congressmen would start coming by for their "bracers." I'd pour them scotch or gin, and often I'd be allowed to sit in the back while the members talked or complained and gossiped (the era of daytime "pops" and "bracers" on Capitol Hill is long gone, but like an episode of Mad Men, that was the way it was back then).

This is truly where I learned the most about the Hill and the people who ran it. Those sessions made up most of my invaluable, real-life education and I wouldn't have traded them for the world. One of my favorite Congressmen, Bob Jones, (D) Alabama, was Chairman of the Public Works Committee. This was quite a powerful position as he was in charge of all the roads and bridges and other such public works, often known as "Pork." (There is some uncertainty as to where the term "pork barrel" originated, but most likely it was linked to the pre-Civil War practice of giving slaves a barrel of pork salt as a reward but letting them determine how it would be split.) Jones had a thick Southern drawl / mumble which made him indecipherable at times. Jones would amble up to the front desk of Thompy's office quite often and in garbled dialect say, "Is that no-good, tricky member of yours here?" Thompy would yell out, "Come on in!" and Jones and Thompy would drink and carry on for the better part of an hour. The first time I came in to pour Jones his "pop," I was wearing a loud, seventies-style shirt with bright patterns and colors on it and he looked me up and down and said, "What Guinea you steal that shirt off of, boy?"

Jones was outspoken, colorful and quite a character and he would come up with memorable quotes. In the early seventies, school busing was being implemented by the Federal Courts to integrate the public school systems, so students were literally being bused across town. Parents of white students were extremely upset about the situation and many were coming across the bridges from Virginia to protest this practice. When Jones received word of the protestors, he came in to

Thompy's office even earlier than usual for his "bracer," and warned, "Thompy, you know about this busing shit? Better watch out. There are a lot of jumped up citizens coming across that bridge."

Thompy was a popular member of Congress, well-respected and admired by Democrats and Republicans alike. For instance, one of his best friends was John Ashbrook, an extremely conservative Republican member from Ohio. Even though Thompy was a liberal and Ashbrook today would be considered a member of the Tea Party, they were very close friends. They had different outlooks on life, and politically were polar opposites, but they got along well and never let their differences get in the way of a strong friendship. They used to debate labor issues around the country and would mutually agree on who got to win, depending on which part of the country they were in. I used to love it when lobbyists visiting Thompy would assume that Thompy disliked Ashbrook because of their contrasting political views. Ashbrook was trashed by the lobbyists so much in Thompy's office that all of the staff began referring to him as "Trashbrook." By assuming that Thompy disliked Ashbrook simply based on their opposing political views, the visiting lobbyists spoke ill of Ashbrook, and in doing so, offended Thompy instead of winning points. It was a lesson that I would take with me throughout the rest of my career.

As an intern, I was fortunate to be exposed to a lot at a very young age. In the summer of 1972, Thompy became head of the Democratic National Committee (DNC) voter registration drive, and as such, we began to work out of the Watergate the summer it was famously broken into. Kiddingly, we would comment that the Republicans did it, not knowing how correct we actually were. Thompy had run the National Voter Registration Drive for Kennedy in 1960 and the DNC hoped that he could repeat that successful effort on behalf of their presidential standard bearer in 1972, Senator George McGovern of South Dakota. He brought Duffer and others to work with him as staffers, and we worked down the hall from the campaign manager, a relatively unknown political activist named Gary Hart (who would eventually become a U.S. Senator from Colorado and a candidate for President, whose campaign flamed out after the married Senator was pictured with an attractive young woman on his lap in a boat called Monkey Business). The chemistry was bad between Thompy and the McGovern staff. I was not privy to everything, but was quite aware that there was a lot of street money that needed to be distributed and the separate camps could never quite agree on how much or where the money was to go. Thompy resigned from the position and as we were leaving the Watergate offices, he admonished everyone to, "Take everything that's not bolted down. No footprints."

Interning involved a lot of running errands, driving to Thompy's District, and per the boss's instructions, "keeping your eyes open and your mouth shut." Most tasks were mundane, but parts of the job were a lot of fun, especially when a visit to the office of Charlie Wilson, (D) Texas, was required. "Texas Charlie," who would become famous in the movie "Charlie Wilson's War" starring Tom Hanks, ran a front office that looked like a hookers' convention. The movie was about a swashbuckling, womanizing Congressman from Texas who took it upon himself to arm people who were then regarded as the Afghan Freedom Fighters. His congressional district was in the heart of the "Bible Belt," yet somehow he continued to get overwhelmingly reelected despite his lifestyle. He was a member of the Appropriations Committee and oftentimes Thompy would send me to his office. This was welcome duty since the front office looked like a parody of a whorehouse. There were girls with big hair, big boobs and short skirts. A testament to this is a famous quote from Wilson who said, "You can teach 'em to type but you can't teach 'em to grow tits." Charlie Wilson was one of the great characters ever to work on the Hill, and a visit to his office was cherished by every intern.

Driving to the Congressional District, centered in Trenton, was always an education. Sometimes Thompy would meet with labor guys for a "pop" at his condo and they, in turn, would bring contributions, in cash, which would go in the trunk of the car. Usually a trip to Trenton would include lunch at Lorenzo's, which was the political hangout. Being New Jersey, the table discussion would revolve around who had just gotten out of the slammer, was going to the slammer, or who was destined to make a visit there. Some things never change: Governor Chris Christie brags that as the U.S. Attorney for seven years he convicted or secured guilty pleas from 130 New Jersey politicians for fraud, bribery, tax evasion and other charges.

Sometimes Thompy would work the ethnic bars, Polish, Italian, etc…with one of us going ahead at each stop to give the bartender a few bills so that when Thompy arrived, the bartender would announce, "This round's on Thompy!" We would also make the rounds of the city churches to make "donations." Street money was the coin of the realm for all sorts of religious and ethnic groups, and in those pre-Watergate days, it was also quite legal.

After working for Thompy for one year, he told me that he would fire me unless I went back to school, so I did. First I finished my undergraduate degree and then went to law school at American University to obtain my Juris Doctorate, while continuing to work for him. Often picking up Thompy in the evening at The Democratic Club, I became aware of a lobbyist who spent a lot of time there and at the Monacle, another Capitol Hill hangout, and always had an open tab for any Congressman or staffer who wanted a drink. As *The Washington Star* newspaper would later report, "He was a free spender who picked up the check for anyone who happened to be in the bar – when Daryl sprayed the bar, he sprayed the whole bar." There was something unsavory about him and Thompy was cautious around him for this very reason. Daryl Fleming was his name and he was the lobbyist for Kellogg Company.

"Outside of the killings, Washington has one of the lowest crime rates in the country."
Mayor Marion Barry – Washington, D.C.

"I haven't committed a crime, what I did was failed to comply with the law."
David Dinkins, former New York City mayor, on accusations that he failed to pay his taxes.

Chapter 2

When the head lobbyist goes into the Witness Protection Program, it's a bad spell for the company. Kellogg was having a very bad spell. Not only was Daryl unsavory, he was venal. As one lobbyist familiar with Daryl put it, "If there was a legal, legitimate way to do something, and there was an illegal way, Daryl would choose the latter. That's just the way he was." In the early and mid-seventies, Daryl was leading the high-rolling life of a D.C. lobbyist, while I, on the other hand, was finishing college and law school, under threat from Thompy to do so or be fired. In 1973, Daryl resigned from Kellogg Company and went into business for himself. However, before leaving, he secured a $250,000 contract from Kellogg to represent them in D.C. Unbeknownst to him and Kellogg Company, a Justice Department/FBI criminal justice strike force was investigating organized crime's infiltration into the federal government and they had Congressman Dan Flood, (D) Pennsylvania, his administrative assistant Steve Elko and Daryl Fleming in their crosshairs. The investigation was headed by a crack Justice Department prosecutor named John Dowd.

The House and Senate Appropriations Committees have a reputation for being the ultimate "favor factories" because they dole out money. Congressman Dan Flood was one of the "cardinals:" inside the beltway nomenclature for one of the twelve subcommittee chairs of the House Appropriations Committee. A former Shakespearean actor, pencil-thin with a wax moustache, he looked like someone out of another era, and was justifiably called "Dapper Dan." His Subcommittee on Labor Health and Welfare cut a wide swath in the federal budget, which made him someone the agencies he funded had to aggrandize. If he called in a request for a grant or program, he got their attention because he controlled the budget and, thereby, their existence. He could manipulate the agencies' activities to the benefit of his patrons. According to federal prosecutors, Daryl, on behalf of a wide array of interests such as trade schools, trucking companies, rice growers and insurance companies, would bribe Congressman Dan Flood and his administrative assistant, Steve Elko, to affect the decision as to who or what companies were awarded grants from the relevant agencies. They were very successful in delivering "when bought," but the sheer scope and breadth of the criminal enterprise meant it was only a matter of time until there was a crack, and it was Daryl who cracked. The Feds wanted Congressman Dan Flood and to get to him they needed Daryl. If Daryl would turn and start talking, he would become an unindicted co-conspirator and, more importantly, be placed in the Witness Protection Program to protect him from the retribution of the mob and other key players. This was a legitimate concern since, according to the press, the investigation had expanded to "scrutinizing links between D.C. lobbyist Merle Baumgarten who was found dead in an automobile accident two years ago and Capitol Hill restaurant maitre'd Alex Goodarzi who was shot to death." According to the prominent, now-defunct *The Washington Star*, Daryl Fleming had been "placed in protective custody by the justice department and was giving the government detailed information about illegal campaign contributions and had identified individuals and activities here linked to organized crime."

Enquirer & News, Fri. June 24, 1977

Former Battle Creek resident reported informant in probe of Mafia and ICC

By DOUG UNDERWOOD
Gannett News Service

WASHINGTON — Daryl Fleming, a former employe of the Kellogg Co., apparently is a central figure in a U.S. Department of Justice probe investigation of illegal campaign contributions and the infiltration of organized crime into the Interstate Commerce Commission, the Washington Star has reported.

Fleming reportedly is supplying justice's organized crime and anti-racketeering Strike Force with information in its investigation of whether the mob made contact with ICC officials and sought inside information on trucking decisions.

The Star quotes sources outside the government as saying that Fleming is giving such sensitive information that he may been placed in protective custody at his own request.

George Franklin

Enquirer & News. Tues. 10-4-77

Former Kellogg lobbyist gets immunity from federal prosecution, paper reports

Gannett News Service

WASHINGTON — A former lobbyist for the Kellogg Co., who has emerged as a central figure in an investigation of organized crime's links with the Interstate Commerce Commission (ICC), has been given complete immunity from prosecution in return for his cooperation, the Washington Star reported Monday.

Daryl Fleming, held in protective custody by the U.S. Department of Justice since March, made the agreement April 25, but it was not disclosed publicly until late last week, when he testified for the first time at a trial in Los Angeles.

The plea bargaining agreement he signed says Fleming, 46, promised to provide the government with a complete disclosure of organized crime influence at the ICC and the Department of Housing and Urban Development (HUD)

Congressman Dan Flood eventually resigned from Congress in disgrace. A jury voted 11-1 to convict him of five bribery and three perjury counts. The one holdout was the subject of a jury tampering investigation. Before his second trial he pled guilty to one count of conspiracy and was sentenced to one year probation. Steve Elko went to jail. Daryl Fleming, after entering the Witness Protection Program, has, to my knowledge, never been seen again. Meanwhile, as Daryl was supposedly looking after Kellogg, the company had become subject to an anti-trust proceeding that

18

threatened to break Kellogg into three separate entities, and the Federal government began an initiative to ban advertising to children which could cripple one third of the company's business. Kellogg desperately needed a lobbyist.

*"Things are more like they are now
than they ever were before."*
Former U.S. President Dwight D. Eisenhower

*"Washington is a city of Southern
Efficiency and Northern Charm."*
John F. Kennedy

Chapter 3

In the corporate world, one constantly hears the refrain, "Why can't the government run like a business?" I'm not sure which company this references, but there are plenty we don't want the government to emulate. Enron, Tyco and AIG are not exactly paragons of virtue and good management. The reality is, companies rely on competence, responsiveness, integrity and are influenced by the nature of their business, geographic location, the vagaries of the market, and most importantly, leadership. In the mid-seventies, Kellogg was in need of new leadership and a cultural change to adapt to a political landscape that had been evolving while Daryl was supposedly on watch. Daryl was an aberration: Kellogg had always been a conservative, almost insular company, protected from takeover by the ownership of the Kellogg Foundation. The internal path to leadership started by working one's way up through the sales force, peddling ready-to-eat cereal and side items such as Kellogg's® Pop Tarts® and Eggo® waffles. The nature of the company, and even its location in out-of-the-way Battle Creek, Michigan, led to a business-as-usual approach. Employing Daryl made Kellogg executives think it was involved in the world of government relations. It wasn't. One of the more important things a lobbyist can do is give the company a feel for which way the political winds are blowing. If confrontation can be anticipated or avoided, there is nothing to fix. It would take new management and leadership by a Brooklyn-born cornflake salesman to recognize this and instill a culture of genuine involvement. William E. "Bill" LaMothe was an unlikely candidate to change the politically insular culture of Kellogg. He had no past political or public affairs background and was conservative in outlook. He had come up through the ranks the Kellogg way. He was a cereal salesman in Brooklyn, New York, became a Product Manager at Kellogg's headquarters in Battle Creek, took on a variety of corporate projects, and then eventually became President and CEO. Bill LaMothe had a good political antenna which allowed him to see the aforementioned problems for what they were: toxic. Unlike his predecessor and many business executives, Bill LaMothe understood the political significance of an ongoing antitrust case called Shared Monopoly and the attack on advertising to children. His predecessor looked at them as merely distractions that would eventually go away.

The same year Bill LaMothe was made president, by design Dr. Gary Costley was made Director of Public Affairs with a mandate to create a department that could effectively deal with the changing political dynamics. His job: take on the Shared Monopoly Case, and hold at bay any attempt to limit advertising to children. Gary had a PhD in nutrition and biochemistry from Oregon State University, and had been thrown in to the Washington world with Daryl while he was still plying his trade. Gary knew quite well the unsavory side of lobbying, experiencing D.C. from all of the angles. He was discerning and able to look at D.C. lobbying with a jaundiced eye, based on what he had seen during his apprenticeship with Daryl. He was also quick to separate the showbiz aspects of lobbying, of which there is much, from the practical. Lobbyists like to impress their company colleagues with how many people they know. Over the years Gary would admonish me saying, "I don't care who you know, I want to know who will do something for us." It is a distinction with a significant difference.

Further rounding out the new public affairs function would be Peggy Wollerman. A striking blond with a degree in nutrition from Ohio State University, she was to be the public face of the company where consumer groups, legislators, analysts and the press were concerned. All of these groups were part of her constituency. She provided substance and an image that was consistent with the Kellogg of Middle America and as far away as possible from the carnage Daryl had left.

Gary Frink is an unforgettable man: jazz drummer, lawyer and K Street restaurant aficionado, he worked out of a spacious rented home on the part of Massachusetts Avenue known as Embassy Row. Gary Frink looked, dressed and acted the part of a D.C. lobbyist and he knew Gary Costley through Daryl. He and Daryl had worked on some projects together, but conducted separate businesses. Gary Frink was actively promoting the building of the Alaskan pipeline on behalf of Alaskan interests and would periodically get calls on Kellogg-related matters. With Daryl's absence from the scene, Gary Costley's calls to Gary Frink increased dramatically.

After graduating from law school, I asked Thompy for a legal position on one of the committees, but he astutely directed me to look for work off The Hill, advising that even with a law degree, I would always be seen as the go-for. I was getting kicked out of the nest. Enter Gary Frink. He was a one-man show, but with Kellogg and the Alaskan pipeline activity accelerating, he needed someone to knock on doors, attend fundraisers and work the staff, which is what new lobbyists do. I was hired to do just that. If you are a twenty-something lobbyist or Capitol Hill staffer, your professional and social life are inextricably intermingled. It was LinkedIn before there was LinkedIn. We lived it instead of pushing a computer button. Who you dated, who you partied with, whether you played softball, golf or tennis, all impacted who you knew, and thereby the access and knowledge you had. It was a constant swirl that to outsiders appeared exciting, but was actually quite tiresome. Every new acquaintance begins with, *"Who do you work for?"* The degree of interest was determined by political gain. Everything was scrutinized through the lens of the politics of D.C.

I was learning the life of a young lawyer/lobbyist working for Gary Frink and there were a couple of things I needed to do while trying to get established. At the top of my list was to stay involved with political campaigns, so in 1976 I volunteered and went to Atlanta as part of Jimmy Carter's Presidential Campaign Legal Team which, upon his election, provided me access and connections into that administration. I also had started doing work for McDonald's and the National Soft Drink Association, and as such, was carving out a niche in the food industry. Around this time, the United States Department of Agriculture (USDA) was forming a Human Nutrition Advisory Committee which had representatives from business and consumer groups. Gary Costley decided to try to have me appointed as one of the business representatives on the committee. I obtained the support of McDonald's along with some other companies and my name was presented to the Department of Agriculture. The Assistant Secretary of Agriculture at the time was Carol Tucker Foreman, former head of the Consumer Federation of America, and according to my friends at the USDA, her response when my name came up to be the business representative was, "That little son of a bitch, never!" A price to be paid for doing a good job on behalf of the business community, which also prompted Gary Costley to remark, "You must be earning your money if she dislikes you that much." I called Bill Cable, an old friend who was then head of Congressional relations for the House side in the White House, and asked if he would look into it for me. He then called the Secretary of Agriculture Bob Bergland and told him that he had been hearing from all sorts of liberal members of the House: Bill Ford, (D) Michigan; Mo Udall, (D) Arizona; John Brademas, (D) Indiana, etc... and they all wanted me appointed, as did the White House. The Secretary, upon hearing I had this type of support, promptly appointed me to the Committee. When I called Bill Cable to thank him, he relayed to me what had happened. I responded, "But Bill, none of those people called you." To which he replied, "Yeah, I know. But they would have if you had asked them to." That's how things sometime work in D.C.

Working with Gary Frink was going well, but once again Daryl Fleming reared his ugly head. The fact that Gary had been working with Daryl was not lost on the Justice Department strike force. Shortly after I started working for Gary, the Washington papers started carrying news articles about the investigation, and sources inside the Justice Department laid out the specifics of who, what, where and when. *The Washington Star* did a series on the investigation. Daryl was talking not only to the prosecutors, but also to the press. The articles featured stories about Kellogg and relationships that only he knew. My job in those pre-email days was to grab the papers, fax them to Bill LaMothe, Gary Costley and Peggy Wollerman who would then be able to respond to whatever the press was reporting. I in turn would head out to the Hill where the image of Kellogg was taking a beating and, as the de facto Kellogg presence in D.C., I tried to answer the oft-repeated question: "What the hell is going on?"

A strategic leak is an arrow in the quiver of every prosecutor and Gary Frink, having been in Daryl's orbit, made him a tempting target. So it was not surprising, but no less unnerving, when on October 3, 1978, *The Washington Post* ran a story implicating him in the Flood, Elko, Fleming sordid affair. Implicated, not charged, a significant distinction. However, guilt by association in a reputation/image-driven town may be enough to motivate one to start talking, and if the Feds can get you talking, there is no telling where it might lead. They were obviously trolling for information and using the media as their cudgel. Their weapon of choice was making our clients, especially Kellogg, uneasy. Enter "Rockville Tommy."

Tom O'Malley was a savvy lawyer who, like a good Irish bartender, had heard and seen it all as a former prosecutor and criminal defense lawyer in Rockville, Maryland, hence the moniker, "Rockville." He had a feel for politics as well as law (his son is now Governor of Maryland) and the combination of skills made him perfectly suited to help us work through this prosecutorial fishing expedition. The Feds wanted their investigation targets to overreact, so Rockville went into client management mode while he entered into discussions with the prosecutors. The talks were short lived, the Feds had no case. Sure Gary Frink knew Daryl, Elko and Flood, but so did probably hundreds of other lobbyists and when it came down to it, Gary had not been part of their criminal scheme. In other words, he was innocent of wrongdoing and the Feds' interest quickly evaporated.

Finally, Kellogg's Daryl-generated public relations nightmare was over and we now could turn our attention to the Shared Monopoly anti-trust case, a case which threatened the existence of the company.

"Once a man has held public office, he is absolutely no good for honest work."
Will Rogers

"Before I give you the benefit of my remarks, I would like to know what we are talking about."
The Wall Street Journal quoting a Michigan legislator

Chapter 4

If a government agency decides it is going to undertake an initiative rendering one third of the current U.S. economy illegal, it probably should be careful to figure out which industry with which to start. It was with this in mind that the Federal Trade Commission (FTC) chose the cereal industry to test the novel legal theory of a Shared Monopoly. The theory was that Kellogg, General Mills and General Foods "shared" a monopoly, and that they had a "tacit understanding" that kept cereal prices high, and that they moved in lockstep to keep competitors out of the market. According to *The New York Times*, "the case could set the anti-trust precedent for the attempts to break up companies in automotive, steel, electrical goods and various other industries dominated by a few large corporations." The doctrine "success must be punished" was in play. We now had the theory of "too big to succeed." The theory was simply that, a theory, with no law to support it. Ironically, the late Senator Phil Hart of Michigan, for whom one of the Senate office buildings is named, had been chairman of the anti-trust subcommittee and for years had introduced legislation limiting "industrial concentration," which was another way to say shared monopoly. This legislation had never gone anywhere, but, by its mere introduction, implicitly recognized that there was no law behind the theory. Not to be deterred by the law or lack of legislation, the FTC decided to create case law, and their internal deliberations centered on who would be the easy target. "We picked the cereal industry because they lack the political clout to muddy the waters," opined one of the lead FTC attorneys in a *Newsweek* magazine article. Here was an admission that was on point with what Bill LaMothe and his team had known in their gut: that this was as much about politics as it was about the law. The problem was that LaMothe's predecessor, Joe Lonning, and Kellogg's general counsel, Norm Bristol, had looked upon this issue as a straightforward and solely legal proceeding, instead of considering the political aspect as well. They hired the firm of Cravath, Swaine and Moore to litigate the case and neglected to institute concurrent political activity.

Bill LaMothe and Gary Costley knew that this had to be a two-front war, legal and political, and went to New York to meet with Cravath to devise a two-front strategy. Cravath thought that lobbying was beneath them, and in a condescending tone, explained to LaMothe and Costley that the law firm and the law firm alone would take the case all the way to the Supreme Court if necessary. They were sure to win in court; the Kellogg higher-ups should go back to Battle Creek and simply let the lawyers handle the issue. Not a good move by Cravath. They had, with East Coast arrogance, underestimated the grit of LaMothe. He fired them in the middle of the case, which is unheard of in the silk stocking legal community. Since Cravath was not willing to include a political front to the effort, LaMothe was going to replace them with a no-holds-barred, flamboyant street fighter named Fred Furth.

Cigar, cowboy hat and booming voice, Fred Furth flew into town on his own Sabreliner jet from San Francisco. Having made millions as a plaintiff's anti-trust lawyer, he was not a member of the clubby, D.C./East Coast bar, and he relished being an outsider who didn't give a damn what the East Coaster or beltway insiders thought of him, so long as he won the case. He was theatrical and liked to categorize the proceedings in terms of war: for example, "Battleship Kellogg" took hits but was able to continue fighting. The political front was just another theater of war, a theater that eventually proved to be the undoing of the Shared Monopoly case.

Gary Costley, Gary Frink, Peggy Wollerman and I were in charge of the political front, while Fred took charge of the legal proceedings before the Federal Trade Commission's administrative law judge, Harry Hinkes. Realizing some extra firepower would be needed, we brought in the firm of Williams and Jensen with the principle partner, J.D. Williams, without question one of the most influential lobbyists in D.C. Like Fred, he was also armed with a cigar, but his shtick included a good ol' boy paunch, Southern drawl and a knack for being quite entertaining. If a new client was sitting in the office, J.D. would call a Senate office and bellow into the phone, "Senator, J.D. here, we need to talk about this blah blah issue." It didn't matter that it was only a befuddled intern on the other end of the phone who had no idea what he was talking about. As J. D. would later point out, "Clients like to think that you are talking to the Senator." He was best known for his Democrat connections but, like most lobbyists, prided himself on his ability to work both sides of the aisle. This attribute was best evidenced by his response to *The New York Times* when asked how the change in the Senate from Democrat control to Republican majority would affect him, "We are ready for anything but a military coup and give us 24 hours and we will be ready for that."

Politically, we realized a direct frontal assault on the legitimacy of the Shared Monopoly case would not work, but rather we would need a stalking horse until an opening occurred that would allow us to inflict real damage on the FTC. Our horse was a bill called the "Shared Monopoly Moratorium," which called for a cessation in the agency activity until Congress was able to determine the validity and legality of the underlying anti-trust theory. It was introduced in the House and Senate by Representative Howard Wolpe and Senator Don Riegle, both Democrats from Michigan. We knew the bill would never pass, but it gave us a chance to rally constituent groups, seek co-sponsors, and foster doubts about the scope and ramifications of the proceeding by the FTC.

Ironically, given the nature of the case and the premise, we worked in lockstep, but never could come up with a political strategy with General Mills and/or General Foods. General Foods seemed to take a "leave it to the lawyers" approach, while Mills' top government relations officers, Bob Bird and Austin Sullivan, were politically engaged, but not willing to sign onto our stalking horse approach. We couldn't even agree how to end the damn case, much less agree on how to share an entire market!

We decided that we were going to go it alone. As President Lyndon B. Johnson remarked one day when asked about the shape of the earth, "Flat or round, I can teach it either way." That was our approach as we targeted various audiences. With the Shared Monopoly Moratorium bill in place, we set out to generate media support and co-sponsors. We went to St. Louis, Tampa, Tallahassee, Portland and just about anywhere and everywhere we could meet with editorial boards, columnists, or interest groups. The Kellogg union, the American Federation of Grain Millers AFL-CIO, was on board out of enlightened self-interest, so we had the union lobby our Democrat friends, while we promoted the virtues of free enterprise and "don't punish success" to our Republican potential allies. We also began to muscle company suppliers to contact members of Congress because a Kellogg broken into pieces was clearly no longer going to be the customer with the fat checkbook with whom they had been used to dealing. Our approach with suppliers and members of Congress was that of gentle pressure applied relentlessly, and eventually we started to get traction with rice growers in Louisiana, corn in Indiana and Illinois, sugar, both beet and cane, in Florida, Minnesota and Hawaii; and wheat in the Plains states. Members of the House and Senate signed on as co-sponsors as a sop to the constituents, knowing the bill was merely symbolic. We, in turn, kept pounding the marble halls of Congress, waiting for an opening, or a miracle, or a mistake by the FTC. Finally, it came on the proverbial silver platter. After more than two years of taking testimony, the presiding Administrative Law Judge (ALJ) on the Shared Monopoly case, Henry Hinkes, announced that he was going to retire, but that the litigants should not be concerned in that he had reached an arrangement with the Commission to continue the case. Fred Furth pounced. What was meant by an "arrangement" and what were the details to continue the case? He immediately filed a Freedom of Information request seeking all pertinent documents which in turn disclosed an agency hell-bent on continuing the proceedings, to the extent that they eliminated any chance of summary judgment or impartiality by giving the judge a financial interest in continuing the case. As one Hill investigative staffer stated, "Basically the FTC procured a judge like a piece of meat." Judge Hinkes was to be paid as he completed "tasks" usually at the rate of $10,500 per "task," but he also could be fired at any time by the commission "for the convenience of the government." We now had a judge who had a financial interest in keeping the case going but who also could be fired at any time, without cause, by the prosecutor i.e. the FTC. Making this even more egregious, the contract was personally approved by the chair of the Federal Trade Commission, Michael Pertschuk.

Per *The New York Times*, we began to "prowl the halls of Congress," with justifiable indignation over the "Hinkes affair." In doing so, we came across a very junior Democrat member from Michigan named Don Albosta. A low-key, non-descript member, he was clearly in the cul-de-sac of his career, but he was nonetheless a member on the House Post Office and Civil Service Committee, and had two sharp energetic staffers, Micah Green and Charlie Erhlich, who could spot an issue with political legs. Michigan, Kellogg, Post Office and Civil Service Committee, was an unusual, but beneficial combination of factors for him and them. The Albosta team convinced the Chairman of the Civil Service Investigative Committee to hold a hearing on the Hinkes affair. Chris McNaughton, who was then the General Counsel of Kellogg, testified before the committee, stating that the contract had "destroyed Administrative Law Judge Hinkes' judicial independence, creating conflicts of interest between him and the respondents and otherwise created both the appearance and the fact of impropriety and bias." The FTC floundered in response, conceding in a statement that the arrangement was unusual but claimed nothing in the agreement was illegal. It was also clear that the Hinkes affair was becoming something substantive that could affect the outcome of the case. Even the FTC recognized the problems this could cause, prompting one FTC official to opine, "It would be a shame to have to lose, or re-try a case that we are winning." We now needed to do three things: create more media around Hinkes, insert the case into the Presidential campaign and turn up the heat on Capitol Hill.

It was also during this phase that I joined Kellogg Company as Director of Government Relations and became a one-person D.C. office. Life was simple. In essence, I had one policy objective. End the anti-trust case.

Thompy liked to use the phrase "nervous as a whore in church," which pretty well summed up my feelings in the spring of 1980, when I walked to the offices of *The Washington Post* to meet with a young business reporter named Merrill Brown. In that era, if *The Washington Post*, *The New York Times*, and/or *The Wall Street Journal* addressed an issue, it was a big deal and it made the issue real. I became aware of Merrill Brown through his byline, and with a cold call, asked him if I could come see him about a story I thought he would find of interest. Feeding a story in D.C. is routine, but it is fraught with danger. Once one ignites the fuse with a responsible, conscientious journalist, who Merrill was, all control is lost as the journalist will then take the story wherever it leads, warts and all. In our first meeting, we talked for an hour and I described the case chapter and verse, the issue, the politics, the personalities, and the Hinkes affair. He took copious notes, and asked a few questions, all with a skeptical demeanor. We parted on a friendly, professional note, but I left with no idea of what I had just launched, if anything.

Elections are a prime time to get politicians to say and do things they might not normally say and do, especially if the company is located in the swing area of a swing state like Battle Creek, Michigan. The Reagan campaign was the ideological soul mate of our position: Our shared message was, "Don't punish success, eliminate extensive government interference in the marketplace and cut back on regulatory authority." Complete simpatico with our case, and with the Grain Millers Union on our side, candidate Reagan was pro-business and pro-labor at the same time. Now if he would only take a stand against the FTC. Networking our story in his campaign at the national, state and local levels became my part-time job. We continued to knock on doors on Capitol Hill for the Hinkes affair, but began to apply the same fervor to the Reagan campaign citing the merits of our position and the flaws in the Shared Monopoly theory. We needed him to speak out and corner the opposing Carter/ Mondale campaign to do the same. It became clear that the most likely path to success was through networking at the local level, as opposed to starting at the national campaign headquarters. Our incumbent Democratic Congressman, Howard Wolpe, who had introduced the Shared Monopoly Moratorium bill, was aggressive on our behalf in the Hinkes affair. His Republican opponent was a wealthy businessman named Jim Gilmore, who was a lackadaisical campaigner but had significant financial resources. Wolpe, always more liberal than his constituents, was running scared in a marginal District as he always was, and one of the central issues of the campaign was who could do more to end the case, save thousands of union jobs and the company. In countless meetings with Gilmore and his staff, we described how Wolpe would be reeling if they could convince Reagan to come out against the case. We implored and pleaded with Gilmore who understood and agreed. Nothing happened. Meanwhile, Merrill was working his sources. I would get calls from the Hill staff, lawyers and other lobbyists, whom he had been interviewing or fact-checking. This went on for weeks with no story. He was clearly working on it in a methodical, meticulous fashion, but what we didn't know was his timing or the take of the final product.

Finally, on Sunday, July 21, 1980, the article we had been waiting for appeared and in a way we had never imagined. The entire front page of *The Washington Post* Business and Finance section was dedicated to an investigative piece entitled, *"FTC Snap, Crackle, Pop, Storm Over Cereals."* Out of the shoot, the article called the Hinkes affair a "complex and somewhat confusing tale of how the FTC kept Hinkes on board," with a contract "approved by the FTC chairman Michael Perstchuk, a contract largely viewed by the federal management officials and others as an improper, illegal deal." The article went on to describe in great detail the discussions and developments which went into the execution of the contract, citing the "best and worst of Congressional lobbying efforts." The article also went on to say that cereal makers had taken the case to Capitol Hill and that letters directed at the FTC were coming in from "House and Senate members with special interests in cereal production, districts with Kellogg's facilities or districts with financial contracts with cereal manufacturers." We now had national attention and the FTC was in damage control trying to defend the indefensible. *The Washington Post* confirmed our accusations and gave credence to our indignation.

Sometimes what seems so easy and obvious is actually unattainable. We were still waiting for a statement or letter or pronouncement from the Reagan campaign on the case. Finally, frustrated, we gave up. The effort went dormant, but then we learned that Ronald Reagan was planning to visit Battle Creek and his campaign asked me if Kellogg could arrange for Tony the Tiger to greet him as well as former President Gerald Ford who would be joining him. I took the opportunity to reiterate our request with the advance team that if he didn't mention our case the whole visit might veer negative since the Shared Monopoly case was THE Federal issue in Battle Creek. We got their attention. A couple of days prior to the stop, I received a call from Sally Dempsey, Bill LaMothe's administrative assistant, saying that she had just received a letter to Mr. LaMothe from Ronald Reagan stating:

George Franklin

RONALD REAGAN

October 29, 1980

Mr. William E. LaMothe
President and Chairman of the Board
Kellogg Company
235 Porter Street
Battle Creek, Michigan   49016

Dear Mr. LaMothe:

During the campaign, I have attempted to address specific local
issues as well as the broad national issues which affect our
economy. One such issue which is both national and local in
scope is the eight-year-old "shared monopoly" case which the
FTC brought against the cereal industry.

I would like to join with Jim Gilmore and the Michigan legislature
in their criticism of the FTC for ever bringing this action and
needlessly jeopardizing the livelihoods of thousands of workers.
Once again, the federal bureaucracy has expanded the power of the
government, thereby adversely affecting the health and success
of free enterprise through excessive regulation of the marketplace.
It was never intended that the FTC would have the authority to
order a company to divest its assets and thereby restructure an
entire industry under Section 5 of the Federal Trade Commission
Act.

Not only has the FTC exceeded their legislative mandate, but they
have done so with callous disregard for the impact their actions
will have in human terms. I agree with the AFL-CIO that "the loss
of 2,600 jobs of cereal workers who are members of the Grain Millers
and of the Retail, Wholesale and Department Store Union" is an
"entirely unacceptable result."

Specifically, I would support legislation which prevents the
FTC from becoming the arbiter of consumer tastes and preferences.
It is clear to me that the case under consideration has very little
basis in fact and that a favorable ruling on behalf of the FTC
would have a chilling effect on American industry. Thus, I would
support legislation which would narrow divestiture authority
under Section 5 and would detail specific remedies available to
the Commission under that section.

The need to enforce economic competition should be firmly grounded
in the nature of the market-place and not be based on some vague
theory which would seek to establish a "new economic order."

901 South Highland Street, Arlington, Virginia 22204

Paid for by Reagan Bush Committee. United States Senator Paul Laxalt, Chairman Bay Buchanan, Treasurer.

We were ecstatic! The likely in-coming President of the United States had come out against the case and we kept our part of the bargain by beaming the news to every major media outlet in Michigan. The Wolpe camp went into a scramble. Wolpe's Chief of Staff, Jim Margolis (now President Obama's media adviser), called me with a "you SOB" type opening, to which I responded that they just needed to get the Carter/Mondale campaign to take a similar position. Mondale, in a whirlwind series of campaign stops, held a press conference at the Battle Creek airfield the day before the election at which he spoke out against the case. It was too little, too late.

Presidents have a lot of power, but even the newly elected President Reagan could not halt the anti-trust proceedings before the FTC, which is an independent regulatory body. The FTC is directed by five commissioners and until Reagan was able to appoint some new commissioners, the liberal consumer advocacy of the commission would continue. So we kept pressing. The day after Jimmy Carter left the White House, Bill Cable, who had been the head of Congressional Relations in the House for the Carter administration, boarded the Kellogg corporate jet for a day in Battle Creek. Bill had joined the Williams and Jensen law firm and now was working on the Shared Monopoly case with us. It was a pleasant twist for me, since having been Bill's "go-for" on the Education and Labor Committee, I was now his client and we were about to set out on a new strategy to end the case.

Bill Cable carried with him years of Hill political experience. He had been brought in to salvage the widely discredited mess of the government relations under the first two years of the Carter administration and now he rounded out the Kellogg team with J.D. Williams, Gary Costley, Peggy Wollerman and me. The case dragged on and after countless meetings and discussions, we decided to pursue the lobbying equivalent of the nuclear option: we would try to cut off the funding for the case.

In the world of Congress, there are authorizers and appropriators. Simply put, authorizers create the law which provides for the actual existence of agencies and what they are empowered to do. Appropriators, on a yearly basis, fund those agencies, and in doing so, determine what they can and cannot do with those funds. The Shared Monopoly Moratorium bill had been directed at authorizers. Now we would use the Hinkes affair to stop the case in its tracks. Liberals, conservatives, Republicans and Democrats all agreed the Hinkes contract did not pass the smell test, but cutting off the funding for an ongoing Anti-Trust case would be precedent-setting. We would need a stalwart willing to put a "rider" into the FTC Appropriations bill that would cease all funding for the case until the matter involving the administrative law judge Harry Hinkes was resolved. It could be done in closed-session, i.e. it would not be open to the public, but its impact would eventually be loud and very public. We decided to approach a junior Republican member of the FTC appropriations subcommittee from South Carolina, Carroll Campbell. J.D., who usually supported Democrats, had become friends with

Campbell, a Republican, when he first ran by agreeing not to support Campbell's opponent. Campbell was green, conservative and brash enough to take on the FTC. He agreed to do it and in doing so, completely blindsided the commission. The subcommittee bill, which usually stays intact through the process, came out with a provision preventing any further funds from being spent on the Shared Monopoly case until the Hinkes affair was "resolved," but included a not-so-subtle direction that money could be spent to dismiss the case. Now it all had hit the fan. The agency came to Congress pleading that the provision be removed, but its credibility was suspect and the Shared Monopoly case and other activities had created the perception of an agency out of control. Their other activities such as trying to regulate funeral homes and used cars, left the agency susceptible to criticism, and members of Congress were tired of trying to defend the agency from a plethora of constituent complaints from the business community. The Hinkes provision passed the House as part of an overall bill.

George Franklin

97TH CONGRESS
1ST SESSION **H. R. 4169**

IN THE SENATE OF THE UNITED STATES

SEPTEMBER 10 (legislative day, SEPTEMBER 9), 1981

Read twice and referred to the Committee on Appropriations

AN ACT

Making appropriations for the Departments of Commerce, Justice, and State, the Judiciary, and related agencies for the fiscal year ending September 30, 1982, and for other purposes.

1   *Be it enacted by the Senate and House of Representa-*

2 *tives of the United States of America in Congress assembled,*

3 That the following sums are appropriated, out of any money

4 in the Treasury not otherwise appropriated, for the Depart-

5 ments of Commerce, Justice, and State, the Judiciary, and

6 related agencies for the fiscal year ending September 30,

7 1982, and for other purposes, namely:

14   FEDERAL TRADE COMMISSION

15   SALARIES AND EXPENSES

16   For necessary expenses of the Federal Trade Commis-

17 sion, including uniforms or allowances therefor, as authorized

18 by 5 U.S.C. 5901–5902; services as authorized by 5 U.S.C.

19 3109; hire of passenger motor vehicles; and not to exceed

20 $1,500 for official reception and representation expenses

21 $71,958,000. No funds made available to the Federal Trade

22 Commission pursuant to this Act shall be used for the pur-

23 pose of preparing or issuing any initial decision in the admin-

24 istrative proceeding identified as Docket No. 8883. This limi-

25 tation shall expire 60 days after the Commission makes a

1 decision on the recommendation of the Independent Adminis-

2 trative Law Judge on the pending inquiry ordered by the

3 Commission on February 13, 1981. This limitation shall not

4 prohibit the completion of such inquiry nor the dismissal of

5 Docket No. 8883.

44

Elections have consequences, and in 1981, after the advent of the Reagan revolution, Republicans took a majority in the Senate. Now Pertschuk and the FTC's liberal defenders in the Senate were in the minority, replaced by conservative Republicans distrustful of government agencies. This provided a perfect ideological mix for us on the merits of the case as well as the Hinkes affair. Congress had changed and the political mood of the country had changed and now the commission was to change with the appointment of a new chairman, James Miller, a free-market, pro-business Reagan appointee. Miller was the ideological opposite of the consumer activist Perstchuk. Armed with a Ph.D. in economics from the University of Virginia, he was a disciple of the Center for Study of Economic Regulation at the American Enterprise Institute. He had entered government in order to stop the type of initiatives instituted by Pertschuk with the Shared Monopoly proceedings. Hinkes and the sheer scope of the undertaking had taken a huge political toll on the agency, creating an internal squabble among the commissioners, with Miller pushing to drop the suit and Perstchuk wanting to forge ahead. In the end, the vicissitudes of the case and the political climate convinced the other moderate Republican commissioners to part ways with Pertschuk, and with a 3 to 1 vote in 1982, the group voted to drop the case. As one of swing commissioners commented, "To carve out new cereal companies from the hides of existing ones, was just too Draconian."

"If you agree with me on 9 out of 12 issues, vote for me. If you agree with me on 12 out of 12 issues, see a psychiatrist."
Ed Koch, former Congressman and Mayor of New York City.

"I can't be bought, but I can be rented."
Senator John Breaux, D, LA, after committing to vote for the Reagan budget in exchange for the administration's support of the sugar program.

Chapter 5

The two issues which ensure continued employment for food lobbyists are the sugar program and advertising to children. Regardless of which side you are on, these two issues continue to be gifts that keep giving and have put a lot of lobbyists' kids through college. They also have changed the definition of winning and losing. When it comes to advertising to children, not losing equates to winning for companies. As far as the sugar program is concerned, neither side really loses despite the fact that the sugar program continues to this day, which would make you think the sugar growers won. According to the food lobby, however, it wasn't as bad as it could have been, so they declare victory and prepare to wage war all over again when it comes time to reauthorize the program.

The fact that these issues coexist is illustrative of D.C. at work. It defies common sense to legislatively ensure that a commodity be grown while simultaneously discouraging its consumption. However, in D.C., this is normal operating procedure. They also identify a problem, debate and discuss it ad nauseum, with no result. This problem is a result of Congress working exactly as it was designed to work. What does a cowboy from Wyoming have in common with a Hispanic from Tampa? Not much. Yet we take 435 men and women from all over the country, and put them under one roof, take another 100 men and women from all over the country and put them under another roof and expect them to somehow agree with us in how to handle the events of the world and the political and social issues of the day.

The system is designed to govern from the middle. Hence, the apocryphal conversation between George Washington and Thomas Jefferson regarding a bi-cameral legislature, "Why," said Washington, "did you just now pour that coffee into your saucer before drinking it?" "To cool it," said Jefferson. "My throat is not made of brass." "Even so," said Washington, "We pour our legislation into the Senatorial saucer to cool it."

Concerning advertising to children, most people have a visceral aversion to advertising that is directed at children and preteens. But these same people enjoy the benefits of television in the form of an electronic babysitter on Saturday morning and after school. These people argue against advertising to children, but what they truly dislike are certain products, not advertising in general. If Saturday morning cartoons were filled with ads for broccoli, carrots and spinach, we would not be having this discussion, and therein lies the rub. The dissenters want to limit advertising of *content* such as sugar, but there is one major roadblock in their way: the First Amendment.

Michael Moss wrote in his book, *Salt, Sugar, Fat:* "The battle in Washington over sugar began, oddly enough, with a pile of rotten teeth. In 1977, twelve thousand health professionals had signed petitions asking the Federal Trade Commission to ban the advertising of sugary foods on children's televisions shows, and the consumer groups who had joined them decided to add a little theater of their own. They collected two hundred decayed teeth from pediatric dentists, bagged them, and sent them to the FTC along with the petitions for the advertising restrictions." I would argue that the battle dates back even further, starting with a Republican activist named Robert Choate. Testifying before Congress in the early 70s, Choate made a list of the 60 best-selling cereals, and then claimed that 40 of these were nothing more than "empty calories," a term that had, until then, been reserved for alcohol and sugar. Kellogg's Corn Flakes®, Rice Krispies® and Frosted Flakes® were listed among the worst, and, according to Choate, "the worst cereals are geared toward children." *Time Magazine* screamed "Breakfast of Chumps!" The 40-year-long effort to ban advertising to children had begun. Fast forward to the 2012 FTC report on advertising which critically claimed "A comparison of cereal marketed to children and teens with marketing of those same cereal products to all ages reveals that in 2009, the cereals most heavily marketed to children were the least nutritious." Sound familiar? The reason that nothing changes is not for lack of effort by consumer groups. These groups are in the business of being consumer advocates and they need an issue or a cause to justify their existence. When business gets slow, they simply crank up their tried and true "anti-advertising to children" campaign to get their members' and contributors' juices flowing.

Currently, the companies and the consumer groups are still in a standoff, which was proceeded by a full-scale war led by Kellogg's nemesis, the FTC and its Chairman Michael Pertschuk. Perstchuk, who was once described as a permanent storm center, managed to create a full-scale hurricane with his attempt to ban advertising to children. The "kidvid" proceeding, as it came to be called, was a proposed rule promulgated in the late 1970s that would:

1. Ban all T.V. ads geared toward children less than eight years of age

2. Ban T.V. ads aimed at older children 8-12 years, for those sugared products most likely to cause tooth decay.

3. Require those advertisers of all other sugared products to run "counter ads."

The Commission planned to implement this rule under its legal authority to regulate "unfair and deceptive" trade practices, which was a sweeping grant of authority by Congress. Congress granted this broad authority under the rationale that "there were too many unfair practices for them to define." Instead, they would let the FTC define such practices.

Suffice it to say, all hell broke loose in Battle Creek, Michigan; Minneapolis, Minnesota; Hershey, Pennsylvania, and everywhere else kid-dependent food companies were headquartered. This attempted rule embodied the lobbyist's platitude, "Congress can giveth and Congress can taketh away." Such a sweeping definition of unfairness would be the FTC's undoing and the breadth of the undertaking a significant strategic blunder that would cause the initiative to collapse.

On one side of the battle was the ever-deep-pocketed, federally funded FTC, armed with the support of an array of consumer groups including the Food Research Action Council (FRAC), Consumer Federation of America (CFA), Action for Children's Television (ACT) and the Center for Science in the Public Interest (CSPI). The FTC, however, had galvanized an opposition with a huge financial stake at risk. The cereal and candy companies were the face of this opposition, but behind them were the recipients of their vast advertising budgets: newspapers, T.V. stations, broadcasters, ad agencies, toy manufacturers. Free speech advocates rounded out the anti-FTC alliance. Our coalition agreed that our approach was to paint the FTC as an agency out of control, trampling on the First Amendment rights of all the aforementioned entities while becoming, in the words of *The Washington Post* editorial, a "National Nanny." "Kidvid," "National Nanny" and "unfairness" were the buzz words we used as we pounded the halls of the House and Senate office buildings looking for Congressional supporters to remove the FTC's authority to use "unfairness" as a basis for rulemaking. As crazy as it sounds, the far left and the far right were aligned with us. The far right latched onto the National Nanny point as another example of big government run amok and the far left, although kindred spirits with Consumer groups, were concerned about the First Amendment implications of the Agency's proposals. The FTC had clearly overplayed its hand.

Pertschuk and his consumer group allies took the moral high ground, claiming cereal companies were guilty of "moral myopia" and that they had turned children into economic missiles aimed at their mothers' pocketbooks. However, the facts just didn't quite square up with Pertschuk's claim. Was there a connection between sugar consumption and advertising? Did sugar consumption correlate to a disease? When do children really watch T.V.? Don't companies have a Constitutional right to advertise perfectly legal products? Simply put, we pounded the FTC with undeniable facts and reinforced the uncertainty of their plan, along with the adverse economic impact it would have on powerful constituents thus unraveling political support in the House and Senate. Occurring in the midst of already turbulent times for the FTC, the Senate, with 67 votes, approved legislation to end the kidvid proceeding and the House followed suit. They enacted a provision to eliminate the FTC's ability to use "unfairness" for rulemaking, a provision which was later agreed to in conference essentially eviscerating the advertising to children proceeding. Kidvid was dead, or so we thought.

On March 16, 2010, First Lady Michelle Obama spoke to the Grocery Manufacturers of America, where she expressed concern that the average American eats 15 pounds more sugar than they did in 1970 and that our rate of obesity had increased significantly. She went on to say to the major providers of food products to children that we needed to examine "How you market those products to our children," and that parents are undermined "by an avalanche of advertisements aimed at their kids," and that "70% of foods marketed to kids were still among the least healthy." Sounds like a fellow named Robert Choate. The good news is more lobbyists' kids will be able to go to college.

Sugar is not nutritionally beneficial other than providing calories. It also makes food more palatable, but that is about the extent of it. Why then would Congress continue to authorize a program which encourages production at the expense of consumers and to the detriment of the food industry? The answer is very simple: political clout. The American sugar lobby is very good, and despite the best efforts of food manufacturers, consumer groups, free trade organizations, and advocacy groups on the right and the left, they manage to perpetuate a system of limited competition and guaranteed prices double to triple the world price.

The sugar program in its simplest form works like this: the government restricts the importation of sugar, which in turn diminishes the supply and drives up the prices. The program also sets a loan rate for sugar, which allows a farmer to borrow money to grow sugar but if the price of the sugar on the market is not high enough, he or she can default on the loan, keep the money and give the government the sugar. Finally, the USDA is required to purchase surplus sugar for ethanol production, thereby keeping prices artificially high. The program (in practice) is complicated, but the net effect is very simple: sugar growers get very rich, food companies have to pay a lot more for sugar than if they were able to buy it on the open, competitive market and consumers end up picking up the tab. There are approximately 4,700 sugar farmers wallowing in this government largesse to the detriment of approximately 600,000 workers in the food industry. Due to companies moving to other countries such as Canada and Mexico for lower cost sugar, America lost an estimated 127,000 jobs in the food manufacturing sector between 1997 and 2011. We used to banter that the sugar program cost to Kellogg was 50 million dollars each year. You would think with this kind of money on the table, the American food industry, with the support of consumer food groups and other unlikely allies would be able to prevail. Not a chance. Presidents Gerald Ford, Jimmy Carter, Ronald Reagan, Bill Clinton and George Bush have all aided and abetted the program for three basic reasons: the "intensity of the issue," campaign contributions and corn. Let's start with corn.

The sugar program is part of the Farm Bill, which also impacts corn growers. Corn farmers of the Midwest quickly figured out that if they could keep the price of sugar high, they, in turn, would be able to charge more for high fructose corn syrup, which is prevalent throughout the food system as a sweetener. By supporting the sugar provisions in the Farm Bill, the corn growers would help artificially inflate the cost of sugar and make high fructose corn syrup the less expensive alternative; coming in right under the price of sugar, but higher than they would have been able to charge without the sugar program. The political backing for the sugar program includes not only the beet and cane states e.g. Florida, Louisiana, Michigan, Minnesota, etc... but the entire corn belt as well. The Congressional votes for sugar quickly add up.

The sugar lobby also understands the PAC system (which I'll discuss later) quite well and the importance of money. In the 2011/2012 political cycle the sugar cane and beet growers gave $5,309,072 to Congressional candidates split evenly between Democrats and Republicans. This financial support is based solely on their Congressional stance on the sugar program. This allows the sugar program's success despite defying the existing employment, financial and philosophical facts.

As far as the intensity of the issue is concerned, companies such as Kellogg, Nabisco and Conagra have a number of issues for which they seek Congressional support; members of Congress know that if they are against a particular company on sugar, they can help them with another issue. In the legislative scheme of things, sugar growers are really only concerned about one issue: the sugar program. For them, the sugar program is the only thing that counts and they support Senators and Congressmen who will often be totally unreasonable on their behalf, even derailing the legislative train, if that is what it takes to protect the sugar interests. Intensity of an issue always wins, and for 30 years I ducked for cover every time I saw a guy named Joe Tubilewicz, who was in charge of purchasing at Kellogg, because he would immediately ask me, "What the hell are you doing about that damn sugar program?" because I knew my answer was "Nothing."

Sugar as an issue finds its way into nutritional guidelines, school feeding programs, after school snacks and the Women Infants and Children (WIC) program where the sugar limit has a net effect of banning fruit. Yes, you heard me right; healthy fruit, as in raisins.

The WIC program is a multi-billion-dollar federal feeding program which provides vouchers, primarily through state departments of public health, to eligible participants to obtain pre-approved food products to supplement the diets of pregnant women, infants and children. The program affords hundreds of millions of dollars for ready-to-eat cereals but not all cereals are eligible. To qualify, the cereal must contain 45% of the minimum dietary requirement of iron, no more than 6 grams of sugar, and then must be put on an approved list by each state based on cost, availability and popularity.

General Mills dominates the program with Cheerios®. For Cheerios® in the WIC program, General Mills has no marketing costs, no couponing, and no excessive promotion. It is found money. The cereal is placed on a store shelf and WIC participants pick up the familiar yellow Cheerios® box to the tune of a few hundred million dollars a year. This was a market Kellogg needed to crack, but it was a money pipeline General Mills would defend to the death.

Kellogg's® Bran Flakes® qualifies for the program, but its popularity is limited. Kellogg's® Raisin Bran, which consists of Bran Flakes and raisins, did not qualify, since the naturally occurring sugar in raisins causes the cereal to exceed the 6 gram limit. This is ironic since the USDA encourages the consumption of fruit and even runs a raisin program to encourage their production and consumption. The absurdity goes even further. Local and state health departments give WIC participants brochures, which literally recommend adding raisins to cereal. Our cereal was banned for doing exactly what the government was telling people to do. This argument should have been a no-brainer: just go to the Department of Agriculture and request that fruit be exempt from the sugar limit. Not so simple. At this point, General Mills stepped forward to protect the "integrity of the process" which was a euphemism for protecting their Cheerios®-in-WIC cash cow. Enter Tom Jolly.

Tom Jolly is a funny guy and very good at what he does. Like most D.C. lobbyists, he works both sides of the aisle, but he has especially strong relationships and credibility with liberal Democrats, who we suspected would be the most suspicious of what our ultimate motive was for opening the program to Kellogg's® Raisin Bran. We brought on Tom to help, but things got nasty very quickly. General Mills immediately began to arouse opposition through consumer groups and WIC officials by telling them that this was the thin edge of the wedge to open up the program to all sorts of highly sugared products. Their righteousness was palpable. The Center for Science in the Public Interest (CSPI), Public Voice for Food and Health Policy, the Food Research Action Council and the Center on Budget Priorities (all self-appointed guardians of the WIC program) began to scream bloody murder over this attempt to alter the standard of THEIR program. Tom and I started knocking on doors to assuage the concerns being raised in the Senate and the House offices. Clearly, we were attracting attention. In fact, we attracted enough attention so that *The Washington Post* saw fit to write an editorial on this issue:

Raisin Wars - Washington Post - July 30, 1991

THE FEDERAL government thinks that children should eat less sugar and more fruit, which is fine - except when it's contradictory. The fruit that the government likes can be a major source of the sugar that it doesn't. The contradiction arises with particular force inside a box of Kellogg's Raisin Bran. Can you believe that it may now arise within the U.S. Senate as well?

It seems that, were it not for the sugar from the raisins, this product of the Kellogg Co. would be eligible to be bought by needy families under the sugar standard of the government's WIC program, a stern 6 grams per serving and no more. Counting the raisins and the rest of the sugar in the box, however, it's not eligible. That's true even though the same Agriculture Department that maintains the WIC regulations can be found in other contexts urging Americans not merely to eat more fruit, but to put it on their cereal.

Kellogg cares, and not just for love of consistency in the Code of Federal Regulations. The WIC feeding program for needy pregnant women, infants and children is itself a pretty big bowl of breakfast. It helps to feed nearly 5 million people including a third of the nation's newborns at a cost of about $2.4 billion a year. Of that, an estimated $150 million goes for cereal, and about two-thirds of the cereal money, Kellogg says, is spent on Cheerios, which meet the WIC sugar and other nutrition standards and are made by Kellogg competitor General Mills. WIC really stands for women, infants and Cheerios, the Kellogg people like to joke, not sweetly.

Kellogg, based in Michigan, is urging that state's Sen. Carl Levin to offer an amendment to the agriculture appropriations bill somehow relaxing the sugar rule so that the raisins won't count. Other senators including minority leader Bob Dole have warned they will resist a step they call a threat to the program's "integrity." They cite a letter from the American Academy of Pediatrics and other protective groups urging that the question of what can and cannot be bought with the money not be politicized and noting that the department is already in the midst of a regular reexamination of the rules.

If the government is going to cross the threshold of setting nutritional standards at all - as perhaps it had to, at least in the particular kind of program WIC is - we suppose it was bound to come to this. You make the rules, and the next thing you know poor kids can't have Raisin Bran, which other kids are eating without ill effect, because to allow Raisin Bran is to open the floodgates to government subsidized Snickers bars for poor and nutritionally deprived families. It is government at its most famously elephantine. Of this much only we are certain: The Senate floor is the wrong place to write the rules. But the Agriculture Department, if it is to have a free hand, should at a minimum keep the free hand light. Surely it's possible to have rules that square with the WIC program's raisin d'etre and still let in a scoop of raisins.

War, peace, national debt and now Kellogg's® Raisin Bran qualified as editorial-worthy in one of the most prestigious and influential papers in the country.

This debate was only about fruit, not about Kellogg's Froot Loops® or Frosted Flakes®. Michigan Democratic Senator Carl Levin, known for thoughtfulness and fairness, decided to call us into his office along with an opposing proponent, Bob Greenstein from the Center on Budget Priorities to hear firsthand what this kerfuffle was all about. Tom and I showed him handouts from the Calhoun County Michigan Health Department, paid for by the USDA, telling WIC participants to add raisins to their cereal. Greenstein countered to Levin that, "This is only the beginning" of a slippery slope; Levin listened to our debate and concluded the meeting by directly telling Greenstein, "This does not make any sense. I'm with the company on this one." Not all of our meetings went as well. The Hill and Federal agencies operate on, "When in doubt, don't approach." Spread enough doubt and uncertainty, and you can stall anything in D.C. and General Mills and Consumer groups were doing a very good job of just that. It actually got so nitpicky where we were defending the glycerin on the raisins and debating whether or not the "added sugar coating on the raisins" was determinative. General Mills' obfuscate and delay tactics were clearly working, so we decided to throw a Hail Mary pass. We arranged for our then CEO, Arny Langbo, to meet with the Republican (thus supposedly pro-business) Secretary of Agriculture, Ed Madigan. Tom, Arny and I sat down with Secretary Madigan and his aides in the USDA conference room. The press reported that, "Kellogg Chairman Arnold

Langbo started shouting and pounding the table." The press was right. It got ugly very quickly, an adamant CEO colliding with an arrogant Secretary. No one budged.

The USDA continues to encourage WIC participants to add fruit to their cereal, promotes raisins, and Kellogg's® Raisin Bran still does not qualify for the WIC program. In January 2014, President Barack Obama signed a new five-year Farm Bill with the sugar program intact; despite the opposition of food companies, consumer groups and advocacy organizations. *The Wall Street Journal* reported taxpayers are "footing an 80 million dollar bill" per year for the sugar program. Some things never change.

*"The only things in the middle of the road
are yellow stripes and dead armadillos."*
Jim Hightower, former Texas railroad commissioner.

*"There comes a time to put principle
aside and do what's right"*
Michigan legislator according to The Wall Street Journal.

Chapter 6

Holly Hassett of Hershey Foods could recite a list of West African countries and the condition of the cocoa crop. Jane Hoover of Procter and Gamble knew all the political intricacies of banana republics where coffee beans were grown. Ted Smyth of Heinz focused on their new sauces and acquisitions in Indonesia and expanding baby food sales in China. Only a small sample of the issues facing international food companies.

I would become immersed in the more mundane issues of trade, tariffs and quotas, but my initiation into the world of international government relations began with a volatile mix of race, politics, money and oppression. It was called apartheid and involved the repressive government of South Africa, where hundreds of U.S. companies do business. Apartheid comes from the Afrikaner word meaning "the status of being apart," and was a system of government controls imposed in South Africa after World War II, whereby the four racial groups of "native, Asian, white and colored" were to be kept separate. There was Grand Apartheid which designated where people could live, and there was Petty Apartheid which segregated restaurants, hotels and similar public facilities. Unlike in the U.S. during segregation where we feigned "separate but equal," in South Africa the system and objective was "separate and unequal." By all accounts this system worked as planned. Economic and political power was concentrated in the white minority to the almost total exclusion of the other races. Whites lived in plush suburbs with large homes surrounded by walls topped with razor wire. The homes and gardens were tended by blacks who, when their work day was done, returned to designated "townships." In these townships homes often consisted of tin or cardboard lean-tos and one water tap might serve hundreds of families. The idea of indoor toilet facilities was as remote as taking a trip to Disney World. The townships were concentrations of squalor and abject poverty. White versus black, rich versus poor, separate and unequal with no hope for an oppressed majority created a volatile, combustible mix.

Kellogg, like many U.S. companies, entered South Africa after World War II and saw it as a beachhead for expansion in the African continent. The Kellogg manufacturing plant is located in Springs, an industrial town not far from Johannesburg. The product line is very recognizable to U.S. consumers, including Kellogg's

Corn Flakes®, Rice Krispies® and Raisin Bran. The marketing was directed at the white population with disposable income. Our approach was to keep out of politics, sell cereal, and make money. This approach worked fine until the 1970s when Reverend Leon Sullivan, a black minister from Pennsylvania and a member of the General Motors board, decided that adhering to the South African status quo was not okay, and that U.S. companies would have to do more to effectuate change. He initiated what was to be called the Sullivan Code, which required U.S. companies who did business in South Africa to take on philanthropic endeavors and political activity targeted at changing the system of apartheid. Housing projects, school programs and advocacy became part of the cost of doing business. These requirements were accompanied by mandated periodic reports and audits which created an entire micro-industry and bureaucracy due to the demands of Reverend Sullivan. Why didn't Kellogg and other companies simply refuse to go along? U.S. domestic political pressure in the form of consumer boycotts. The African American community in the U.S. was pushing Congress to pass a law ordering all companies to divest of their South African holdings. The Sullivan Code provided a rationale for why the companies should continue a presence in that country. It also served as a buffer against potential boycotts by U.S. African American communities and other anti-apartheid activists. This was an area of great concern to a consumer product company such as Kellogg.

General Motors, Exxon, Ford and almost 200 other American companies in addition to Kellogg signed and began to implement the Sullivan Code, and all of a sudden, Kellogg found itself running with the big boys. Many business experts in and out of the company questioned why Kellogg would take all this heat at the risk of damaging the U.S. business in the name of South Africa, which constituted only a minute one half of one percent of the entire Kellogg worldwide business. There were two reasons: first, we felt deeply that it was the right thing to do. Our mantra was, "We can't change things by remote control;" secondly, then-CEO Bill LaMothe was adamant that we would not leave South Africa until, as he told me one day, "Congress passes a law saying we have to leave." On this issue, he was the CEO equivalent of a heat-seeking missile, locked in, not to be deterred.

Reagan was President of the U.S. at the time and he strongly supported the efforts of the companies to stay in South Africa. However, he was undermined in the Senate not only by Democrats but by Republican leadership as well. It was the activity in the House of Representatives, however, that propelled Kellogg to take on a large role in the effort, much larger than Kellogg's relative South African presence. The Congressional Subcommittee on African Affairs was chaired by Democrat Howard Wolpe from the Third District of Michigan. The District included the corporate headquarters of Kellogg and the Upjohn Company (now part of Pfizer). Dr. Ted Cooper, CEO of Upjohn, was as hell-bent as Bill LaMothe about staying and conducting business in South Africa. Howard Wolpe was a leading, if not THE leading proponent of divestiture. An African expert, his political opponents claimed that he cared more about the third world then he did the Third District. He was as adamant in his position that the companies should leave, as Bill LaMothe and Ted Cooper, CEOs of the two biggest non-government employers in the District, were that they should stay. Sure enough, LaMothe and Cooper decided they wanted a one-on-one with Wolpe to discuss the situation and asked me, along with Ed Greising, my Upjohn counterpart in D.C., to set up a meeting. Ed and I knew there would be no good outcome from this confrontation, but it was pointless to argue with two determined CEOs. We were to organize the collision, let the wreck occur, and then pick up the pieces.

Bill LaMothe, Dr. Cooper and I boarded the Kellogg Falcon jet for the one-hour flight to D.C., where we met Ed for the trip up to Capitol Hill. There was not a lot of small talk. When we arrived at the office, we were told by LaMothe and Cooper they wanted to meet alone with Wolpe, so Ed and I stood outside the office in Wolpe's Chief of Staff, Marda Robillard's, cubicle. The men shut the door to the office and the shouting started quickly. Clearly, these typically thoughtful, low-key individuals had adamant views. Marda looked at us and we looked at Marda, all thinking about those issues and politics other than South Africa where we needed Howard and he needed Kellogg and Upjohn. It was a head-on collision, parts everywhere and few pieces left to pick up.

When Joe Stewart, my boss and Vice President of Public Affairs, Scott Campbell, General Counsel, and I began going to South Africa to confirm the company directives were being enacted and enforced, we were just another U.S. company participating in the Sullivan Code. Our role would increase dramatically, through a combination of Bill LaMothe's leadership, our location in the Third Congressional District of Michigan and our support for Christopher Dlamini, the soft-spoken South African union leader at the Kellogg plant. Our corporate presence in Howard Wolpe's District was noted at the highest levels of the South African government, which gave us great leeway to do things other companies might not even attempt. We were the first to recognize a black trade union, led by Christopher. Such recognition was against South African law, but the directive from headquarters was that Kellogg was going to treat its employees at the plant in Springs just as we treated our employees at the Omaha, Nebraska; Memphis, Tennessee or Lancaster, Pennsylvania plants, regardless of South African segregationist laws. This was fine in theory, but the result in a country with an insurrection/ revolution under way was quite profound.

Mangosuthu Gatsha Buthelezi was the Chief of the Zulu nation, founder of the Inkatha Freedom Party and leader of KwaZulu, the territory set aside for the Zulu people. He was a controversial black leader. Fiercely anti-communist, estranged from the African National Congress (ANC), but most importantly for our purposes, opposed to the divestiture of the U.S. companies. His support for our position was critical as we attempted to fight legislative efforts in D.C. to require divestiture. We had met with him numerous times in KwaZulu and even had hosted a dinner for him in Georgetown with a group of American CEOs. The meetings were meant to shore up his support, as a major black leader, for our refusal to leave. Our last meeting with him turned out to be clearly the most memorable.

Oscar Dhlomo, Chief Buthelezi's top aide, met Scott Campbell and me in the lobby of a hotel in Durban, South Africa. As we entered the elevator to Chief Buthelezi's suite, Oscar casually mentioned that there was some media in attendance to cover the meeting. I thought to myself, this is not good, but we can handle this, maybe some local press. As the elevator doors were about to open, I asked exactly who "the media" was, to which Oscar responded, "*60 Minutes*." Holy shit. Lights, Camera, Action! Sure enough, there stood a cameraman from *60 Minutes* filming us as we walked off the elevator. The filmed conversation with the chief was vacuous, but I will never forget Scott as we sat in the Johannesburg airport the next day waiting to board the flight to return home, telling me there were three good things about our upcoming appearance on *60 Minutes*. I asked him what they were and he replied, "First, we're landing in New York City where there are the most want ads in the country" (implying our need to look for a new jobs); second, "I've fired a lot of people at Kellogg and we fire people great." I asked what the third good thing was, to which he replied, "I'm senior to you, so I have to call LaMothe and you don't." Yes, that was a good thing for me.

Christopher Dlamini was many things to many people. To the South African government, he was a terrorist and a communist. To the African National Congress (ANC), he was a freedom fighter. As far as Kellogg was concerned, he was our union leader of the plant in Springs, First Vice President of the

Coalition of South African Trade Unions (COSATU) and politically engaged, which meant he had a target on his back. Kellogg was worried about Christopher's safety, since this was a time in South Africa when state security forces would abduct "terrorists" from the townships, never to be seen again, and sometimes "accidents" would occur in which the individual "fell out of a window," or "committed suicide." Our concern for him was justified. In early November 1994, I got a call from the Managing Director of Kellogg in South Africa telling me Christopher was missing. We assumed correctly that the security forces had taken him from his home in Kwa Thema, the township in which he lived. He had been arrested under Section 29 of the Internal Security Act and taken to John Voster Square, an infamous prison/detention center at which, for unknown reasons, prisoners had a propensity to fall out of windows and fall prey to similar accidents. Christopher was in great danger.

I informed Bill LaMothe and his reaction was decisive and succinct. I was to get a message to the President of South Africa, P.W. Botha (aka The Great Crocodile) that if Christopher was not released unharmed, LaMothe was going to go out in front of the headquarters in Battle Creek, in the heart of Howard Wolpe's District, hold a press conference and announce that Kellogg was leaving South Africa. I asked Bill if he really wanted me to send such a message. His short unequivocal answer was, "Yes." Talk about high stakes politics. Luckily, through my D.C. and Sullivan Code dealings, I had met the Ambassador from South Africa to the U.S., Bernardus Gerhardus Fourie. After reconfirming that LaMothe really wanted me to pose this ultimatum, I called Ambassador Fourie's office. Shortly thereafter, LaMothe received a call from President Botha assuring him that Christopher would be released, unharmed, which he was. During subsequent trips to South Africa, Christopher would often thank us for saving his life.

The demand was met for two reasons. First and foremost, Christopher was released because South Africa was greatly concerned that sanctions, including divestiture, might pass Congress and they couldn't afford having a high-profile company such as Kellogg, especially one headquartered in Howard Wolpe's District, pull the plug on its business in South Africa. Second, we did it through channels that would not draw public attention and create the perception that South African government capitulated or was weak, a perception which The Great Crocodile would never allow. South Africa would not be embarrassed or lose face.

Christopher's release was a story of both immediate and lasting success. On our frequent trips to South Africa, while apartheid was still in effect but crumbling, Joe Stewart and I would meet with Christopher and he would reiterate that he probably would not be alive but for Kellogg's intervention. Years later when I was with some Kellogg employees in Beijing, I asked them if they wanted to have some fun and go over to meet the South African Ambassador to China. Perplexed, they agreed, and we drove over to a warm reception from Ambassador Christopher Dlamini. After the release of

Nelson Mandela from prison, and the implementation of true democracy in South Africa, Christopher had become a Member of Parliament and then a member of the diplomatic corps serving in China and Mongolia, proving LaMothe's point that you can't change things by remote control.

"Does the chaplain pray for the senators? No, he looks at the Senators and prays for the country."
Two visitors in the Senate Gallery

"There are a lot of mediocre Americans. Don't they deserve representation on the court?"
Senator Roman Hruska (R) of Nebraska on the Supreme Court nomination of Judge Harold Carswell

Chapter 7

My title at Kellogg was Vice President of Worldwide Government Relations. Like most employees in similar positions for large companies, my role was as a sort of company free safety, a football term for a defensive back who covers a wide range of territory and adjusts coverage depending on the play at hand. It is also a position that sometimes opens doors to a world outside of Congress, Presidents and State legislators. This was especially true in September 2001. Everybody remembers where they were on 9/11, as I do, but my most vivid memory was of September 20, 2001. That was the day I accompanied Muhammad Ali to Ground Zero, nine days after 9/11. It was surreal.

A few days after 9/11, I was asked by Carlos Gutierrez, the relatively new CEO of Kellogg to meet with him. He had received a call from Mayor Rudy Giuliani's office, requesting help getting Ali, a member of the Nation of Islam, to New York City, to spread a message of peace and hopefully help damper the heightening anti-Islamic rage. Unbeknownst to most people, even in Southwest Michigan, was that Ali lived in a former gangster's home outside of Benton Harbor, Michigan, just down the road from Kellogg headquarters in Battle Creek. Giuliani's office had connected the dots and asked whether Kellogg could make a jet available to get Ali into New York City for the day. Carlos asked me what I thought about this proposal and I said we should do it. Carlos wanted a Kellogg person on the plane and that person was me.

Early morning September 20, I drove to Battle Creek from my home in Kalamazoo, met Denny Reed and Dale Alexander, the two Kellogg pilots for the ten-minute flight to Benton Harbor, where we were to pick up Ali and his wife Lonnie, along with two of his other associates, Michael Bingham and Michael Constantine, at the Whirlpool corporate hangar. Everyone was ready when we arrived and we all boarded the flight to White Plains, New York, where New York City police officers would meet us to drive us into the city. Parkinson's disease had obviously taken a toll on one of the most famous and recognizable person in the world. I sat in the front seat with Ali and Lonnie, where he tried to eat a muffin, but with his hand shaking, it was difficult to do so without spreading crumbs everywhere. Lonnie was caring and kind and you could see the genuine affection she had for him as she tried to tidy him up as he ate. As we neared White Plains he seemed to get confused as to why we were going to New York City. I addressed him as "Champ" and explained about the terrorists and the attack and the importance of him speaking about Islam as a religion of peace. He hesitated a few minutes and then looked at Lonnie and asked, "They're not mad at me, are they?" She assured him they were not.

Once in New York City, our first stop was a fire station near the World Trade Center where many of the firefighters had been killed and injured. There were mounds of flowers on the sidewalk and palpable grief unlike any I'd ever experienced.

People's reaction to Ali throughout the day intrigued me to say the least. Total strangers, suffering immeasurable loss, would run to him and hug him in tears. He consoled them with a hug but also went through what I learned was a routine where he would have the person put a fist to his chin and have a picture taken of him or her hitting "The Greatest." People swarmed around him, and we tried, unsuccessfully, to keep our emotions in check. The following is *The New York Times* account of our next stop:

> "The press room was oddly quiet at the command center on Pier 92 yesterday until the whir of an electric cart filled the air. Riding on that cart was Muhammad Ali, who came to New York from his quiet town in Michigan to show support for the rescue effort and to show that Islam is a 'religion of peace, not hate.' No one knew he was coming, but there he was, fresh from the fire station, where he re-buoyed the spirits of the firemen. He said that he had been devastated by the disaster, but equally sad that his religion, Islam, appeared to be portrayed negatively. 'Rivers, ponds, lakes and streams, they are all the same,' said the former boxing champion who was disabled by Parkinson's disease. 'They all have different names, but they all contain water. As religions have different names, they all contain the truth.'"

The truth about that scene was that we were emotional wrecks. The walls of Pier 92 were plastered with pictures of lost loved ones and the aisles between the makeshift cubicles were filled with parents, husbands, wives, sisters, brothers and friends in stages of grief and denial, suffering beyond description. They were in emotional hell but like at the fire station, people would come up, and hug and tearfully thank Ali for coming.

Our final stop was Ground Zero. The vision is seared in my memory, but my ability to describe it is elusive. It was as if scripted, a scene out of a movie: a dreary day, military checkpoints with armed soldiers checking to see who went where. Driving through a gray mist in the streets of New York, we came upon what I estimated to be about 13 stories of smoking rubble surrounded by makeshift tents of workers. It was incomprehensible, but tragically real.

The cops, firemen, soldiers and medics would stop and yell, "Champ!" and "I remember your bout with so and so," as we made the rounds and gathered for pictures. It was all fleeting, but important. The world cared about them and what they were doing and hopefully Ali's presence buoyed the spirits of those men and women doing the unimaginable.

Eighteen hours after leaving Battle Creek, I was sitting in my home in Kalamazoo trying to comprehend where I'd just been, what I had just seen and done. I still haven't. I do know that I was very proud of my country, the firemen, the cops and citizens of New York City and the company for which I worked.

Most of the "free safety" activity is dramatically more prosaic than New York with Muhammad Ali. Trade Association meetings are ongoing and if you're in D.C. for Kellogg, whose headquarters is tucked away in a small Midwest city, there is a plethora of go-to-New York trips to represent the company since you are "close." There was usually enough business in D.C., however, to keep one busy. Most days and meetings were nondescript; however, I remember one event quite well, given the setting and with whom I ended up meeting.

Bill LaMothe was quite active in the national program called Drugs Don't Work, (ironically, Dr. Cooper, CEO of Upjohn, a drug company, was also) the gist of which was that through prescreening companies would be able to ferret out would-be employees with drug issues. The White House was solidly behind this initiative along with the usual array of business groups, Chamber of Commerce, National Association of Manufacturers, etc. One day I got a call in D.C.

from Battle Creek that President George H. Bush was going to make a presentation to the Drugs Don't Work organization in the Rose Garden, and I was to attend representing Kellogg. Although I didn't know anything about the program, I thought this was a no-brainer. I would check in, sit in the back of the Rose Garden like you did when you were going unprepared to a college class, and get out of there. I entered the security gates of the White House and went to the event's check-in table. Upon giving my name to the lady, she said, "Oh, you're representing Mr. LaMothe; you have a reserved seat in the front row." "Uh oh. Okay," I thought, "Sit and say nothing and get out of here." So I did. I was sitting between the Chairman of Johnson and Johnson and the Attorney General of Pennsylvania when President Bush came out into the Rose Garden. All was going fine until, at the very end, when the President closed by inviting all of us in the front row to join him in the Oval Office to discuss the program. Now I found myself going into the Oval Office with the President of the United States, on behalf of Kellogg, to discuss a program I knew nothing about. This was not good. I dutifully lined up with the other ten or so who had been invited in to shake the President's hand as we filed into the Oval Office and I noticed that each one would chitchat with him relative to what they were doing to promote the Drugs Don't Work program in their communities.

My only hope was diversion. Then it struck me, George Koch. George was the CEO of the Grocery Manufacturers of America (GMA), our major trade association, and his son Bobby was engaged to Dora, the President's daughter. As I approached the President,

I thanked him for his interest and support for Drugs Don't Work, but then launched into a soliloquy about George Koch, his son, GMA, and basically anything else I could think of. This resulted in an animated conversation about how great the Kochs were and other informal banter. The discussion in the Oval Office turned into a non-event. I reported back to Battle Creek that the meeting was a great success.

"Congress is so strange. A man gets up to speak and says nothing. Nobody listens and then everybody disagrees."
Baffled foreign observer in the gallery of the U.S. House of Representatives

"If Patrick Henry thought taxation without representation was bad, he should see it with representation."
Anonymous

Chapter 8

I was in the Detroit airport one time with my two daughters who were about eight and ten, when I ran into all sorts of people I knew. One of my daughters looked up and asked, "Dad, how do you know all these people?" To which I replied, "If you gave away money, you would know them, too."

As a lobbyist, an integral part of your job is giving away money, almost none of which is yours. You give it to people running for political office with the hope that when they are in office they will do things for you. You can't just give it to them, however. Instead lobbyists partake in a mating process that entails a lot of sitting, standing, drinking and eating. You give your liver and your waistline for the cause.

It is often repeated, "Money is the mother's milk of politics," a quote from the late Speaker of the California State Assembly Jesse Unruh. (Notably, he also colorfully explained the relationship of elected officials to lobbyists as such that, "If you can't eat their food, drink their booze, screw their women and then vote against them, you have no business up here.") The money quote is permanently embedded in the political lexicon, because it is true. It takes lots of money to run for office or, as Will Rogers once said, "It even takes lots of money to lose."

The official numbers by the Federal Election Commission for the 2011/2012 political cycle reports that over 7 billion dollars were spent on elections. The amount breaks down as follows (I have rounded the amounts by a few hundred million here and there):

14 candidates for President: $1.3 billion

1,949 Congressional candidates: $1.8 billion

National, local and state political parties: $1.6 billion.

Federal Political Action Committees (PACS): $2.2 billion (which are Federal PACs of labor, corporations, etc.)

Independent organizations: $1.2 billion

Now, most people would see this as an obscene and corrupting amount of money spent on elections and it is. The sad part is, this astronomical number is post-"reforms," that were implemented after Watergate, when there was essentially no accounting for cash circulating in campaigns. The Federal Election Campaign Act of 1974 allowed and arguably encouraged companies, unions and other interest groups to form Political Action Committees (PACs). These PACs rely on voluntary contributions from employees and members which in turn allows them to contribute to political campaigns with specific amount limitations. The Act also created the Federal Election Commission (FEC) to oversee this new "reformed" system.

What was intended to limit and control money in politics has instead created an arms race. As one House member commented, "If we didn't write the laws, this would all be illegal." Instead of having to overcome the sleaze factor of unsanctioned cash contributions, corporations, unions and other interest groups now needed to "participate in the process." It was practically a civic duty to give money to politicians as PACs began to proliferate with names like x,y,z Committee for Civic Duty, Good Citizenship Fund, Strength and Security Committee and so on and so on. It was in this environment that the Kellogg Better Government Committee (KBGC) was formed in 1975.

Speaking from experience as a corporate lobbyist, raising money is arduous, as you must convince your fellow employees to voluntarily give you money which you in turn give to politicians whom they may or may not like. This in turn leads to two approaches to distributing contributions. One I will call the "save the world" approach and the other is "save the company." For the "save the world" approach, special interests (by the way, corporations, unions, environmentalists, etc., are all special interests as far as I am concerned) give based on a certain philosophy: e.g. conservative Republican, pro-business, progressive Democrats, etc. These types are pretty easy to spot in a FEC report: 80-90% going to one party, with a couple of contributions to the other party so that they can continue to claim that they are bi-partisan.

The "save the company" approach is much more mercenary. As I used to tell the Kellogg Better Government Committee contributors during my annual report, "Boys, I am not a philosophy major, I don't give a damn if you're Republican or Democrat, Liberal or Conservative. All I care is that who we support helps us sell Corn Flakes." As you may have guessed, Kellogg took the "save the company" approach.

Giving money away is where standing, sitting, eating and drinking comes in to play. The first rule of a campaign donation is that you never mail in a check without going to an event. You need to see, and more importantly, be seen. First and foremost, the candidate and, almost as importantly, the staff need to see you so they know you have been "helpful." This will come in handy when you call for an appointment or have an inquiry. What used to be the standard cocktail party has now expanded to breakfasts, lunches and dinners with the more innovative usually being the more costly. It is not unusual to do a breakfast, possibly a lunch or two and go to a few events in the evening where everyone is doing the "D.C. scalp stare" which entails looking over the head of the person with whom you are ostensibly talking to see who else important is coming in to the room. Another part of the ritual is complaining to other lobbyists how many events you have to cover. This, however, falls in the same category as frequent fliers opining on what a hassle travel is but, in reality, they really would miss the "hassle" if they weren't doing it. A full plate of fundraisers becomes a badge of honor in the league of lobbyists.

The fundraising circuit is appropriately named, circuit being the operative word. Similar companies in your industry spread the political wealth across the same committees, so you tend to move in herds of common interest. Food, health, oil: same lobbyists, same incumbents. You re-run the traps on an annual basis so you can create a "presence," provide "access," and stay in the know as to what is going on in D.C. or in the local vernacular "inside the Beltway." Deciding who will receive this civic largesse is derived from an inscrutable maze of committees, PACs and relationships.

Now assuming you take the "save the company" approach, you begin with geography. The headquarters and plant locations will dictate the first swath of contributions inuring to the benefit of the incumbent House members and/or Senators. The advantages of incumbency are significant. You need the hometown solon on your side to establish your base on an issue, and he or she can serve as a springboard to access other members. Even if you decide not to contribute to an incumbent, it is unlikely you contribute to the opponent since incumbents rarely lose. As an aside, despite the low esteem for Congress, incumbents usually win because constituents like their Congressperson; it is the *other* Congress people who everyone dislikes.

Once your home bases are covered, the committee structure in Congress comes into play. There are 20 standing committees in the Senate and 21 in the House with the names and number of Committees changing according to the whims of each new Congress. "Standing" is the term which connotes permanence. This is in contrast to special or select committees, which change from term-to-term. Each standing committee has jurisdiction over a certain area of the government. Depending on your business, some committees will have more relevance than others. Those committees become the focus of your activity, requiring PAC support for "access." Take the food industry for example: the Energy, and Commerce Committee in the House, with jurisdiction over the FDA, is a critical forum for the industry. On the other hand, the Science, Space and Technology Committee ranks well below the waterline of importance for food companies. Correspondingly in the Senate, the Committee on Agriculture has the ability to affect commodity prices, and thus garners the food industry's attention while as a food lobbyist you probably never would grace the door of the Committee on Indian Affairs.

The size of your wallet, i.e. your PAC budget, dictates the breadth of your benevolence and just about how much "good government" you can afford.

The opportunities to "participate in the process" have grown exponentially as the number of PACs has proliferated and an entire world of finance operatives has developed along with them. Not only do candidates have individual PACs, but campaign fundraising is augmented by a series of national party PACs and other entities directed at both the federal and state levels. To further complicate the process, members of the House and Senate need to raise funds for these groups, so you can enhance your relationships with members by adding to their various tallies. Here are just some of the organizations trying to entice you to contribute:

Republican National Committee (RNC)

Democratic National Committee (DNC)

Republican Senatorial Campaign Committee (RSCC)

Democratic Senatorial Campaign Committee (DSCC)

Republican Congressional Campaign Committee (RCCC)

Democratic Congressional Campaign Committee (DCCC)

Republican State Leadership Committee (RSLC)

Democratic Legislative Campaign Committee (DLCC)

Republican Governors Association (RGA)

Democratic Governors Association (DGA)

In addition, you need to factor in leaderships PACs and member-to-member requests.

The old adage is that every House member looking in the mirror sees a Senator and every Senator looking in the mirror sees a President. In this era, they all look in the mirror and see a need for a leadership PAC. Simply put, a leadership PAC is a means by which members of the House and Senate lobby *other* members of the House and Senate who they need in their corner in order to obtain positions of leadership. The Speaker, Minority Leader, Majority Leader, Whip and Committee Chairs are voted into these positions by their fellow members of the caucus and the best way to line up support is to do just what the lobbyists do: give members money for their re-election. The best part: They give away lobbyists' money!

Members fundraising for other members is slightly more subtle than leadership PAC giving, but just as effective. Congressmen and Senators travel the country raising funds from special interests and part of their success depends on their colleagues' ability to help them raise money. If you become a Committee or Subcommittee chair, you are expected to raise money for other members of the Committee or others in need. So, as a lobbyist, you often get calls from a member with whom you are close asking to attend an event for another Senator/Congressperson. Your company may or may not have an interest in the recipient, but that doesn't matter. What matters is that you were there when the calling member needed help, and hopefully he/she will be there when the company needs help. Off to another fundraiser.

Preparation for the onslaught of requests varies among corporations, but it usually has a few common characteristics. Most companies have a committee that oversees the PAC and must approve contributions. At Kellogg, I would submit a list of candidates, ones we knew we would support, for pre-approval at a certain monetary amount. Then, when I received an invitation or a call to support that candidate, I could commit on the spot. This pre-approval would also include some of the major campaign events, e.g. Republican Congressional Campaign Dinner, Senate Democratic Congressional dinners, etc. (the only issue with these events was which member would get credit for selling you the ticket.) The next list would be comprised of "maybe" contributions depending on issues, Committees, etc. People on this list normally required some discussion, which also gave me a feel for whether I could get them approved down the road. Rarely, however, is someone rejected by the PAC committee, since most of the committee members didn't know who these people are to begin with.

Obviously, House and Senate members can't raise all of their funds by themselves, and since it is illegal for their government staff to do so, incumbent office holders have independent finance teams. Non-incumbent candidates also require a finance team, which often is created prior to even formally announcing formation of an exploratory committee. This requisite has spawned an entire industry of consultants and young staffers who hop scotch from campaign-to-campaign as "finance directors." They are nomads who specialize in raising money for campaigns. They will latch on to a Senate, House or Gubernatorial campaign for the duration, while being compensated anywhere from $3,500 to $12,000 per month depending on experience, type of campaign, etc. and then migrate back to D.C. where they will encamp at one of the political committees until the next round of campaigns when they go out into the "field" again. If they hit the big time, eventually, they latch on to one of the 40 or 50 independent fundraising companies in D.C. where raising cash is a for-hire, full-time job.

What have developed are layers of fundraisers. A typical Senator may have a campaign/state finance director and a Washington-based national finance director both of which may be supported by a full-time national fund-raising company. All the players know each other, and share lists from which the members "dial for dollars," this is, make fundraising calls. It is all quite incestuous.

Political fundraising, thanks in large part to the Supreme Court, is a growth industry. The court in a series of rulings since 2007, highlighted by Citizens United v. FEC in 2010 allowing Super PACs and McCutcheon v. FEC in 2014 striking down overall limits on contributions by individuals, have opened the political process to a tsunami of cash. How this will impact fundraising, lobbying and campaigns is unclear, but it is obvious, as *The Washington Post* reports, "The five conservative justices on the Supreme Court seem determined to dismantle the entire edifice of campaign finance law." One sure bet in this ever-changing environment is that politicians, lobbyists and money will remain inextricably intermingled.

*"I don't give 'em hell, I just tell the
truth and they think it is hell."*
President Harry Truman

*"I have been told I was on a road to
hell, but I had no idea it was just a mile
down the road with a dome on it."*
President Abraham Lincoln

Chapter 9

Talking heads and political pundits repeat ad nauseam Tip O'Neill's maxim, "All politics are local." For multi-national corporations it has become a truism that "all politics are international." Kellogg, like most major U.S. companies, is an organization composed of competing facilities throughout the world. The company went "international" when it began selling corn flakes in Canada in 1914 and then went on to build manufacturing facilities in Sydney, Australia in 1924 and Manchester, England in 1938. Kellogg now has manufacturing facilities in Asia, South America, Europe, Africa and North America, all of which compete with one another. Whichever facility achieves the best combination of low cost and quality will get the business to source their part of the world. For example, if Kellogg Australia can make a better product at a lower price than Kellogg Japan, then the plant in Australia will get the business in Asia-Pacific and will service that part of the world. It will also get the financial support from the headquarters to grow and build the business. This is where government relations comes into play.

International government relations, just as U.S. domestic government relations, is an amalgamation of disciplines – law, sales and public affairs – but with an added twist of diplomacy based on the social and political mores of the country. The purpose of the function is the same: persuade the government to do or not do something which benefits the company.

It is self-evident that tariffs and trade restrictions affect cost but what does government relations have to do with quality? Quality and cost are the key corporate determinatives and are complementary components; you have to prevail on both counts to beat the competition, i.e. other plants. Access to affordable ingredients directly impacts the quality of your product, and tariffs are a tool utilized by government to limit access to protected commodity ingredients. Kellogg's battle over corn is a perfect example of this.

Kellogg plants require huge volumes of high quality corn "flaking grits" from which they make their famous corn flakes. We wanted U.S. grits to be available to plants in Mexico, Venezuela, Korea and other plants around the world for both quality and cost purposes; however, these same countries wanted to use their own corn to support domestic business and to protect local farmers and local grain millers. In trying to knock down some of these barriers, I quickly learned that agricultural issues are some of the most politically sensitive around the world.

Cliff Gibbons ate and slept international issues. This is not surprising given his father, Congressman Sam Gibbons, chaired the Trade Subcommittee of Ways and Means. Cliff did a stint at the U.S. Trade Representatives (USTR) office under former Florida Governor Ruben Askew and was steeped in the lingo and the dealings of the trade world. Because of his expertise and tenacity, I contracted Cliff as an external lobbyist to see if he could help us attack some of the cost and access issues affecting the Kellogg plants.

The first thing we had to do was remove ourselves from the big picture of trade issues which are called "rounds," a term used in the trade world to recognize a series of negotiations focusing on certain sectors of the economy. (These so called rounds are usually named after the city in which they began, e.g. Doha round.) They go on interminably. Sheila Page of the Overseas Development Institute once described following trade negotiations as "like watching paint that never dries," which is an apt description. Our job was focused on the relatively narrow world of Kellogg and we didn't really give a damn about the undertakings of the rest of the trade world. All we cared about was corn grits.

Mexico was our first big challenge. Despite passage of the North American Free Trade Agreement (NAFTA) there were tariffs still in place to be phased out over time. Corn, a staple crop of the Mexican diet and a politically sensitive commodity, was at the top of this list with an 8 percent tariff. Now 8 percent may not sound like a lot, but when you are talking about millions of kilos of grits, it is a lot of money even for a company the size of Kellogg.

In an effort to eliminate the tariff, we devised a three-pronged approach. First, we would use the economic/political importance of the United States as leverage with the Mexican Embassy in Washington. Second, we would use Capitol Hill and White House contacts to activate the U.S. Embassy in Mexico City and the USTR on our behalf. Finally, we would attempt to extricate ourselves from other ongoing and contentious bilateral trade discussions then underway between Mexico and the U.S.

No matter how much political clout we could muster, an attempt to open the "corn door" would be a nonstarter unless we could narrow the scope and breadth of its impact. Our approach for this would be a concept called an "end-user provision" which, in our case, meant we would propose that only flaking grits imported "for the production of ready-to-eat cereals" would be exempt from the tariff; a very specific and very targeted request. This would accomplish a three-way win: a win for Kellogg since we would escape the duty, a win for both the U.S. farmers and the Illinois mill that supplied the grits, and finally a win for Mexico which would curry favor with the U.S. and help further the economic expansion of the Kellogg plant in Queretaro, Mexico with minimum impact on their corn farmers and millers.

Embassies act as lobbyists for foreign governments; they wine and dine the U.S. government the way U.S.

companies wine and dine Congress and the Executive Branch. Their lobbying activity as an aspect of their function is quite transparent if you peruse the reports filed under the Foreign Agents Registration Act of 1938 (FARA). This law requires agents representing foreign interests in a political or public relations context to register with the Justice Department. Originally intended to disclose what was perceived to be efforts by Nazi Germany to disseminate propaganda in the U.S. prior to World War II, it has now evolved into a catalog of foreign interests and lobby relationships intertwined in a maze of trade, defense and security.

Take Egypt, for example, which is the second largest recipient of U.S. foreign aid. In the final years of the reign of President Mubarak, Egypt retained the services of former Congressman Toby Moffett, (D) Connecticut, and former Congressman Robert Livingston, (R) Louisiana, to lobby the U.S. government to facilitate the sale of 20 F-16 fighter jets, made by Lockheed Martin, to that country. According to the Sunlight Foundation, Moffett and Livingston also represented Lockheed Martin. The lobby firm was being paid by both the buyer and the seller. Not bad work if you can get it, or as the old politician used to say when accused of conflict of interest, "Doesn't conflict with my interest!"

The more unsavory the foreign government, the more costly the representation will be. Dictators, despots and corrupt regimes as well as international friends of the U.S. and allies retain D.C. lobbyists on a myriad of issues. Somalia, United Arab Emirates, South Sudan, Nigeria, Dubai, Mauritius, Madagascar to name a few, all have D.C. representatives, i.e. lobbyists, who charge anywhere from $20,000 per month to a couple of million dollars per year. Trade, aid and military affairs and armaments are all on the "agenda," not to mention damage control when issues of corruption and coup d'états occur.

Our friends to the south, Mexico, have had a significant presence in D.C. for quite awhile. Just recently, with the election of President Enrique Pena Nieto, the Mexican government hired the firm of Chlopak, Leonard, Schecter and Associates to represent them after having spent roughly $2 million in the last half of 2011 lobbying scattered among an array of Mexican government departments, boards and the embassy.

For our corn plan, the first thing we did was discern which members of Congress had an interest in or special relationship with Mexico. We then took that list and matched it to where Kellogg had existing relationships to determine to whom we would go for help. We then asked members of Congress and the United States Trade Representative (USTR) to express an interest on our behalf when we went to meet with the Ambassador and/or Commercial Officer of Mexico on our proposal. This initial foray evolved into the format we used in other countries to obtain things we wanted or needed and when combined with the right amount of persistence, proved to be quite successful.

Fortunately for us, the U.S. Ambassador to Mexico was former Congressman Jim Jones, (D) Oklahoma.

Steeped in politics, he had been the youngest Chief of Staff to any U.S. President, having served in that capacity under Lyndon Johnson, and had finished his Congressional career as Chairman of the House Budget Committee. The Mexican government knew he had clout back in D.C., and he knew how to get things done. He also was a close friend of the Gibbons family, which gave us an unmatched entrée.

On our first trip to Mexico City, the Ambassador asked us to join him for dinner at a local restaurant. Cliff and I arrived first and were escorted to a table in the rear of the dining room. Soon, a series of black SUVs and sedans arrived. The Ambassador bounded out of his car, surrounded by machine gun-toting security. Two guards covered the front and back doors with a few more guards roving the grounds. I kept looking out the window at the security, all the while trying to concentrate on the conversation at hand, but finding it was very difficult to focus, considering the small army in place to protect us.

Ambassador Jones gave us sage advice on both substance and process and in doing so laid out a road map of whom to see both in and out of government. Working with his staff, which helped us make our appointments and sometimes accompanied us to meetings, we completed a series of discussions with Mexican trade officials, corn interests and economic development entities. We kept our focus narrow: eliminating the tariff on flaking grits for the production of ready-to-eat cereals.

It took a few trips to Mexico City and quite a few visits to the Mexican Embassy in D.C., but finally a deal was struck. The Mexican government would "accelerate" the tariff reduction under NAFTA to 0 percent duty for our specific purpose. It had taken more than a year to accomplish, and quite a bit of traveling, but the savings for Kellogg would be millions of dollars from year-to-year for the next few years until NAFTA was fully implemented.

Once we prevailed in Mexico, word spread to Kellogg's country Managing Directors around the world and they began calling to increase their plants' competitiveness within Kellogg's manufacturing world. Venezuela, Korea, Ecuador, Thailand all had requests which we tried to fulfill. Not all of our attempts were successful, but we were able to win a few using the Mexico playbook. We also had created a new work stream for Kellogg's Government Relations.

Sometimes "international" relations can also involve domestic issues, as was the case with our importation of Kellogg's® Mueslix® cereal from Canada. Mueslix® was an Americanized version of muesli, a very popular European breakfast cereal containing some uncooked grains, as well as fruits and nuts. Kellogg's® Mueslix®, a variation of the original, also contains some uncooked grains, which according to U.S. Customs, put it into a different and higher-tariff HS category than ready-to-eat cereal. (HS is the abbreviation in tariff nomenclature for the Harmonized Commodity Description and Coding System, developed and maintained by the World Customs Organization to synchronize duty rates and categorizations.) According to U.S. Customs, the uncooked grains rendered Mueslix® as a not "ready-to -eat" cereal, but rather a commodity classified like wheat, corn, etc. The problem with this determination was that it didn't pass the "Hee-Haw" test. It was ready-to-eat and this illogical customs determination was costing Kellogg well into seven figures by putting it into a tariff classification with a higher rate.

Kellogg's Legal Department unsuccessfully challenged the customs ruling and was planning an appeal when we in the Government Relations Department became aware of the controversy. To us, the solution was a rather simple: change the law. The lawyers were perplexed, "What do you mean change the law?" Just that, take our case, which in this instance was a bowl, a spoon and a box of Mueslix®, to the Congressional Ways and Means Committee of Congress, share with them a bowl of ready-to-eat Mueslix® cereal, and ask them to the change the law regarding the Mueslix® classification.

Our first stop, however, was a visit with George Weise, Commissioner of the U.S. Customs Service. We were accompanied by recently retired Congressman Sam Gibbons. Commissioner Weise had been Staff Director of the Ways and Means Subcommittee on Trade of which Sam had been Chairman. Let's say they had a solid relationship. After pleasantries and a general description of the issue, Sam whipped out a bowl, poured in some Mueslix® and milk and handed the Commissioner a spoon with the suggestion he take a bite. Sometimes, common sense does prevail in government. Commissioner Weise had the General Council on the phone within minutes with a directive to draft a bill which would place Mueslix® in the category of ready-to-eat cereal.

After 12 to 15 bowls of cereal with members and staff of the Ways and Means Committee, we had a consensus that the existing determination of Customs, although arguably technically correct, defied common sense. Our legislation was included in a package of noncontroversial technical connections which sailed through the House and Senate. The Kellogg refund check was a million-plus dollars, a nice return for the cost of those few bowls of Mueslix®.

The Kellogg experience in the International arena and the handling of the Mueslix® issue highlighted two aspects of the U.S. corporate government relations functions. First, the reality is that government relations is often an orphan in the corporate structure, due partly to the fact it is an amalgamation of disciplines, but more to the fact that U.S. businessmen, unlike their European and Asian counterparts, are never taught or exposed to government relations as an integral part of doing business. Illustrative of this disconnect was a statement by with Andrew Liveris, CEO of Dow Chemical in the September 6, 2011, *The Wall Street Journal* when questioned about his role in the political arena and development of economic policy: "I grew up with Dow in Asia, and in Asia working with governments is the way things get done. People like me in business are very used to going into the corridors and talking with governments about what they need for job creation …

. As I go around the world, public policy is on my agenda – lowering trade barriers, getting consistent energy policy treatment, working with governments to do joint ventures, like in Saudi Arabia and Brazil. <u>The intersection of government and business is almost complete" (emphasis added).</u>

Undergraduate and graduate business programs do not teach government relations, even though most major companies have a Government Relations Department just like they have Finance, Tax, etc. If you are a food company, your largest customer is probably the federal government, debunking the common conception that Wal-Mart is always the biggest corporate customer. Factoring in food stamps (now called Supplemental Nutrition Assistance Program [SNAP]), WIC, school feeding programs, the military and a grab bag of other programs, I would argue Uncle Sam is probably numero uno.

Additionally, Government Relations is misunderstood in the corporate structure because it falls in the gray area between Legal and Public Affairs. Lawyers are taught process and procedures. Lobbyists, as was the case with Mueslix®, exist to circumvent traditional process and procedure, and this dichotomy can create tension. Public Affairs professionals often are not used to dealing with the law or parsing words necessary when drafting legislation or dealing with agency regulations and activity. As a result, in my Kellogg career, Government Relations went from Public Affairs to Legal and back to Public Affairs and back to Legal. It was truly the gypsy of corporate functions.

International Government Relations isn't only tariffs and trade. Cliff and I were involved in some of the first Kellogg forays into China when Kellogg was considering building a plant there. Once again, we were lucky in that the U.S. Ambassador Jim Sasser, a former U.S. Senator from Tennessee, was also a political friend who knew Kellogg and the role the company played in his home state.

I will never forget the time I accompanied Senator Sasser on a tour of the Memphis plant when he was up for re-election. It was during the time of the Federal Trade Commission shared monopoly case, and out of the corner of my eye I saw a burly union worker crawling over the machinery coming towards him. I thought to myself, oh my God this guy is going to duke him out. This union guy got in front of him and bellowed, "Senator, just want to tell you something. You go back to Washington and tell those sons of bitches to leave this company alone! I make more money than I ever dreamed of making and my father worked here before me and made more money than he ever dreamed of making and we don't need a bunch of bureaucrats screwing this place up!" I couldn't have scripted it better.

As was the case with Ambassador Jones, Ambassador Sasser counseled us on how to best position our company politically for the needed Chinese approvals for what would hopefully be a new plant. This was especially delicate in China where the lines between government, banking, industry and the Communist Party are blurred; they are separate, but intertwined. We dutifully met with representatives of all of those entities, but after three or four days of circular discussions we were advised by the U.S. Embassy staff that it was time to meet with the State Planning Committee and they secured us a meeting.

The Embassy provided us with a car and a driver who quickly got lost on the way to the meeting and, in so doing, we discovered that another car had been following us. We asked the driver who he thought that might be and nonchalantly the driver responded that it was probably members of the Communist Party. At this point, we concluded that we were lost and suggested that our driver ask the Communists tailing us how to get to the office or the State Planning Committee. He did and what ensued was like a scene out of a movie. They led us through a series of back alleys to what appeared to be a dilapidated warehouse with a massive metal door. The building was beguiling. Opening the door was like entering the Emerald City. We were met by beautiful carpets, magnificent antiques, paneled rooms and ceremonious greetings. Finally we were about to meet with top officials.

The Chinese officials were gracious, attentive and inscrutable. We never confirmed what role our activities had in securing approval for the plant in China, which was secured shortly thereafter, but I imagine the process we went through was integral to success in the opaque system of China. Somehow, through a confluence of lawyers, lobbyists and business negotiations, Kellogg got its Chinese plant.

Pirated knock-off goods are a way of life in China. Ironically, their presence is so blatant that one of the main street fairs for knock-off watches, cell phones and everything imaginable is right outside the U.S. Embassy in Beijing. Kellogg cereal was not immune to this knockoff culture.

Shortly after we began production in Guangzhou, counterfeit Kellogg's Corn Flakes began to appear on

Chinese grocery store shelves. They were good copies as far as the packaging was concerned. They were good enough that I used to keep a box of "Chinese" Corn Flakes on my desk in Battle Creek and people would stop by to see what they thought was product we were producing in China. The familiar rooster was there, along with Kellogg's red logo on the front. The problem was that it wasn't our product. The only packaging difference was that the imposter's label claimed 11 vitamins and minerals and our product only listed 9.

So like any American company, we sued in the local Chinese court system to stop this egregious counterfeiting activity. You would think it was an open and shut case, right? Not in China. The Court ruled against "US" and fined "US" using some sort of contorted logic to defend a corrupt system. Our only chance for relief was to get the case transferred out of the local province to Beijing. To this end, we enlisted the assistance of U.S. Trade Representative Mickey Kantor. Trademark and patent infringement was an ongoing sore spot between the U.S. and China and Kantor saw Kellogg's Corn Flakes® as a clearly identifiable consumer product that could illustrate the need for the Chinese government to crack down. With the world watching, Ambassador Kantor held a press conference regarding piracy and trade in Beijing with Kellogg's Corn Flakes® in hand as the prop; we finally had the attention of the Chinese through CNN.

The Chinese government intervened and had the case transferred to the Capitol. The court in Beijing ruled in our favor and ordered that the counterfeit plant be shut down. After the ruling, the counterfeiters came across the room and, with unmatched chutzpah, asked if we had any interest in buying manufacturing equipment because they weren't going to need it anymore. Needless to say, we declined.

"You will get the vote of every thinking person."
Reaction to a speech by Adlai Stevenson

"Not enough, I need a majority."
Adlai Stevenson comments to his
supporter after that remark.

"Blessed are the young, for they
shall inherit National Debt."
Herbert Hoover

Chapter 10

Securing an insatiable demand for economic incentives, commonly referred to as corporate welfare, has been the new growth area for government relations over the past couple of decades. The masters of this burgeoning field are the National Football League team owners. They adroitly combine civic pride with the possibility of an economic renaissance as the rationale for why taxpayers should give hundreds of millions of dollars to billionaires to build a factory, a.k.a stadium, so that twenty-two millionaires can run around a field eight times a year, while wealthy fans from the suburbs watch. The civic leaders argue that if you lose them it is the end of Gotham as we know it! The fact that the Cowboys don't play in Dallas, the Redskins don't play in D.C. and the New York Giants don't even play in their namesake city/state, is somehow irrelevant to the conversation. The teams are seen as critical to the city's economy.

Baseball, hockey and basketball are not far behind in their impudence. The audacity award, however, goes to the Detroit Red Wings of the National Hockey League. The Red Wings are owned by Mike and Marian Ilitch who by all accounts are very fine people, but that is not the issue. The issue is that the City of Detroit is bankrupt. It takes on average an hour for police to respond to a 911 call and 40 percent of the street lights don't work, yet the taxpayers are going to ante up $283 million as part of a new $450 million arena. In addition, the Ilitches get 100 percent of all arena revenues from tickets, concessions, parking, etc., so the city actually loses $7 million a year they used to get from these sources from the old arena. Sheer madness!

Gretchen Whitmer, a Democratic leader in the Michigan State Senate remarked, "If you want people to live in the city and not just go to the games, you have to invest in schools and have the police respond to calls. There are so many investments that should trump a sports stadium."

Oh well, at least they have their priorities straight. Who needs street lights, police protection, pensions and health care when you have hockey!

Now, routine economic incentive activity does not garner the same amount of publicity as do major sports leagues, but it does involve the same mix of politics, lobbying, law and crony capitalism and the fact that we use the word "routine" tells a story. It used to be getting an incentive was an extraordinary and noteworthy event. Now it is so routine that NOT getting an incentive, as was the case with renovation of Chicago's Wrigley Field, is a newsworthy event. As Harry Graver commented in the July 29, 2013, *The Wall Street Journal* article, "Remarkably, in an era when teams regularly blackmail cities and states for new stadiums or major renovations – pay us or we'll leave – the Cubs plan to foot the entire $500 million tab."

Since it is routine for a company to seek an incentive "package" when they build a new plant or make major investments, it has spawned a new industry to shepherd companies through the process. Law firms, accounting firms, government relations companies and consulting groups have created departments dedicated to assisting companies secure the largesse of government. Often the same captains of capitalism who bemoan government interference – CEOs, Chambers of Commerce and manufacturing associations – are the very ones advocating for continued and expanded incentive packages. When called to task for not fulfilling the jobs or investment commitments, they are also quick to claim that the government just doesn't understand the free market system. As Rob Crabb, Director of State Tax Policy for Kellogg used to quip, tongue in cheek, "Those pesky bureaucrats."

Getting money from the government is not as easy as it may seem. There are necessary steps to follow and requirements which must be met before the taxpayers start writing companies checks. Critical elements include, among others:

1. Financial incentives by state or local governments are given based on the company's capital investment in the local area and/or creation of new jobs and the anticipated impact on the local economy. These jobs may be actual new jobs or full-time equivalents.

2. There must be interstate competition. Can the project go elsewhere? Has the company looked at sites in other states?

3. A "but for" aspect. Meaning that "but for" the incentives, the investment would not occur.

4. Applications must be filed with local and state government authorities and eventually publicly disclosed. This aspect often requires appearances before public bodies explaining the project and the requested assistance.

Sure, working with government can prove tiresome, but the benefits of found money make it worthwhile. They may include:

1. Cash grants
2. Real and/or personal property tax abatement
3. Job tax credits
4. Job training
5. Hiring assistance
6. Energy cost reductions
7. No interest or low interest loans
8. Infrastructure improvements

Most of these incentives are acquired through negotiations in which the line between what is private and public becomes blurred, especially relating to infrastructure. This can be illustrated by a time when Kellogg executives toured a potential manufacturing site with then-Governor Ned McWherter of Tennessee who was known as "Bigfoot." During the tour, the Governor took the cigar out of his mouth and asked me, "What is it you really need?" To which I responded, "It is not a lot, but what we really need is a road from here to that highway for access to the plant." The Governor turned to the State Director of Transportation, who was part of the Governor's entourage, and asked him, "What do you think?" The Director responded with an eye-glazing, mind-numbing explanation of different road programs, fundraising sources and difficulties associated with all of them. Finally after a few minutes of this, Bigfoot removed his cigar, looked at the Director and barked, "Build the road." Our CEO, Bill LaMothe, who was standing next to me, leaned over to me and whispered, "I like this guy."

Once an incentive package is agreed to, groundbreakings, ribbon-cuttings, press announcements ensue. This brings many people, some of whom who did nothing, out of the woodwork, confirming the old adage "victory has a thousand fathers." Then the hoopla ends and the mundane takes over. Reports must be filed, dollars spent and jobs created to fulfill the commitments made that warranted all the tax breaks and benefits which accompany the incentive. If not, the dreaded "claw back" kicks in, a term which makes company executives squeal like stuck pigs. It simply means that if the company does not fulfill the promises made (such as the number of new jobs created and dollars spent to benefit the local economy) the company has to pay back the benefits received and forgo additional funds in the future. Sounds fair, doesn't it?

"What do you mean payback the benefits?!" "Don't they understand the free market system?" "They need to work in the real world." I have heard them all from company officers complaining over the audacity of government types wanting the taxpayer's money back. "Those pesky bureaucrats."

"When are these good people going to go home?"
**Senator Paul Coverdell to his Chief of Staff as
constituents congregated in his D.C. office.**

*"You know Congressmen are the nicest fellows
in the world to meet. I sometimes really
wonder if they realize the harm they do?"*
Will Rogers

Chapter 11

Most people don't get fired before they get hired, but I was able to accomplish that feat through a combination of Presidential politics and one bad decision. In October 2004, the Presidential campaign was in full throttle and Battle Creek, in the midst of a swing part of a swing state, was at the center of campaign focus. President George W. Bush was campaigning in Southwest Michigan via bus and was holding a rally at the local baseball field. The chairman and CEO of Kellogg at the time, Carlos Gutierrez, always had an interest in politics, but had never been especially active. As a Cuban American, he was keen on issues affecting Cuba, but was also a pragmatic businessman who did not let his personal politics affect his responsibilities to the business, a trait often missing with CEOs. An example which illustrates this concerns the Kellogg Mexican leadership team who wanted to participate in a trade show to be held in Cuba. They nervously called me to express their interest, but also their concern for how Carlos, as a Cuban American, would react. They asked me if I would investigate Carlos' feelings on the matter. My office was around the corner from his, so I strolled over and asked Rosemary Johnson, his administrative assistant, for a few minutes of his time. After explaining the Mexican team's concerns, he looked up and said, "If it's legal and they can make money and get paid they should do it."

Despite his prior lack of political involvement, it didn't surprise me when Carlos stopped by my office the morning of the Bush campaign rally and suggested we go out to the ballpark to participate. Knowing that I was a registered Democrat, he quipped, "Don't worry, you don't have to clap too loudly." When we got to the field, we were seated in the VIP section with the local Congressmen, the Mayor of Battle Creek, and other civic and business leaders. The event itself was boiler plate. The President's speech was the same one he gave three or four times a day during his campaign. Afterwards, however, one of the President's staff stopped by the box and asked Carlos and three or four other dignitaries to meet with the President before he moved on to his next rally. I wasn't invited, so I told Carlos I'd wait for him so we could ride back to headquarters together in his car. Fifteen minutes later, Carlos materialized from the meeting and, in the car as we drove back, Carlos mentioned, "I think he offered me a job." To this I asked, "What did he say to make you think he offered you a job?" Carlos responded, "He said something like 'when we win this thing, are you going to join our team?' or something like that." I reacted by downplaying the significance of such a comment saying, "Hell Carlos, he's probably been telling that to all sorts of people all day long."

It is quite common at the beginning of a second term for there to be changes within the Cabinet, which is comprised of the Vice President and heads of 15 executive departments: Defense, Interior, State, Commerce, etc.

Seven other positions also have Cabinet-level rank: White House Chief of Staff, Administrator of the Environmental Protection Agency, Director of the Office of Management and Budget, United States Trade Representative, Ambassador to the U.N., Chair of the Council of Economic Advisors and Administrator of the Small Business Administration. All of these positions, except the White House Chief of Staff and the Vice President, require extensive vetting and Senate confirmation. It wasn't that Carlos wasn't qualified to serve, but it was considered unlikely that someone who had not been a more active partisan would be selected.

I couldn't have been more wrong. A few days after Bush's election, I got a call from Rosemary asking that I come by and see Carlos. As I entered his office, he shut the door and said, "You have to promise me that what I'm about to tell you, you will tell absolutely no one. I've been contacted by the personnel office of the White House and they want to talk to me about becoming the Secretary of Commerce." I couldn't believe what I was hearing. You would have flunked politics 101 if you picked a guy with little to no political involvement and not a major contributor or bundler to be Secretary of Commerce. "You're shitting me," was my dumbfounded response.

The next few weeks were a whirlwind and a blur as the vetting process began. We had to pull together family history and other information for security clearances in preparation for his confirmation hearings, all the while, not being able to tell anyone what we were doing. This was especially complicated for me personally, as I had begun dating a very beautiful, and very Republican woman in Atlanta, to whom I could not explain why now I was suspiciously AWOL every weekend and making numerous calls daily to a woman named Rosemary. Carlos' nomination was finally announced on November 29, 2004, at a White House press conference after which we began to call the Willard Hotel in D.C. home. (One etymological version of the word "lobbyist" has it that during the Presidency of Ulysses S. Grant, favor seekers would wait for him in the lobby of the Willard Hotel, since he liked to frequent the bar there. Personally, I prefer the version of its origins dating back to the physical structure of The House of Commons in England where advocates would meet with Members of Parliament in the lobby.)

In preparation for confirmation hearings, the nominee goes through what are called "murder boards" and makes the rounds to see key Senators. In Carlos' case, the members of the Senate Commerce Committee would conduct his confirmation hearing. Murder boards are the political equivalent of a mock trial in law school. We would meet with the top officials of the Commerce Department in the Old Executive Office Building (OEOB), the large gray building next to the White House. The agency staff would fire questions at Carlos as if he were before the Committee. My job was to feed them questions regarding Carlos' tenure at Kellogg as CEO that might be uncomfortable to answer. The Commerce team did a good job of grilling him. One night after a long session and everyone had left, Carlos and I were standing outside the OEOB and he queried as to what was the best way to get to The Willard, which was on the opposite side of the White House from where we were. My response, "Hell, you're a big shot; we can cut through the White House." We did. It was a good way to get back to the hotel.

I accompanied Carlos and Legislative Affairs staff on courtesy visits in the Senate. The White House Ethics Office had determined that I was not allowed to join the meetings since I was a Kellogg employee, so I waited in the reception area. I would then have to prep him on the way to the next meeting as to what kind of Kellogg relationship may exist with the Senator, his/her constituents, suppliers, etc. I did have permission to join in on calls to Michigan Senators Levin and Stabenow. I probably could have joined with Senator Gordon Smith, (R) Oregon, as well, who was a personal friend of mine before he entered politics, but opted out of caution. Carlos' confirmation hearing was uneventful. The Committee's Chairman, Senator Ted Stevens from Alaska, and Senator Dan Inouye from Hawaii, the ranking Democrat, worked closely together and were supportive, political allies; thus all the questions were softballs. One humorous moment came when one of the Senators referred to Carlos' two attractive daughters who were seated behind him. In response, Carlos remarked, "They are more difficult to manage than the Kellogg Company." Shortly after his confirmation hearing, but before the Presidential inauguration, Carlos was to be confirmed by the Senate and he asked me if I would serve as his advisor/aide in the Commerce Department. I'd never had a desire to return to D.C. in a professional capacity, and was uneasy with the politics and policies of the Bush administration; however, I thought highly of Carlos and assumed it would be interesting to serve politically at that level. In addition, the timing was good for personal reasons and this seemed like an opportunity to move on. I accepted the job offer and resigned from Kellogg Company.

Luckily, fate intervened and I was saved from myself. I told Carlos I would join his team and found a townhouse in Georgetown. I was flying in from Michigan to sign the rental contract when, upon landing in D.C., I received a call from Carlos who sounded quite uneasy. "Where are you?" he asked as my plane was taxiing to the terminal at Reagan National. "I'm on my way to Georgetown to rent a townhouse," I responded. "You need to come over here right away," he replied. Something was clearly wrong. Arriving at The Willard, I went up to his suite where he was alone and visibly uncomfortable. We sat down next to a small table. He said, "We have a problem. I received a call from Andy Card (President Bush's Chief of Staff) and Karl Rove has vetoed you from coming to work in the Department, because you're too much of a Democrat." (I later found out that the former Republican Governor of Michigan John Engler had gone to Rove to complain.) I was surprised, but deep down relieved. I had never truly been comfortable with the idea of being part of the Bush administration and realized that the personal aspects of my decision had clouded my objective analysis of the circumstances. After a moment, I asked Carlos what else Card had said, to which he replied, that Card mentioned if he wanted to contest the decision his only option was to appeal the veto with President Bush. In response to this, I said, "Carlos, I'm out of here. You haven't even been confirmed and you can't start out by trying to roll Karl Rove. Also, if you were to succeed, I would have a target on my back from the first day." Carlos took in my comments and asked what I planned to do next. I told him that I honestly hadn't had a lot of time to think about it, but I would figure something out. I got up and headed to the door to leave and Carlos asked, "You going to be okay?" and I responded, "Carlos, I've had a lot worse things happen to me over the last few years." To this, he commented, "You sure are resilient." To which I responded, "Not a lot of choice. I'll see you downstairs."

It was one thing to get fired before I got hired, but to have it reported in *The Washington Post*, the *Chicago Tribune* and other national papers took it to a whole new level. The news accounts were generally complimentary towards me ("well-liked on both sides of the aisle," "effective"), but factually incorrect; they cited some convoluted theory that I supported candidate John McCain in the Presidential primaries as the reason Rove fired me.

George Franklin

Gutierrez Denied First Aide – Washington Post

By Al Kamen
Wednesday, February 2, 2005; Page A21

If you want a friend in Washington, as President Harry S. Truman
so aptly observed, get a dog. Incoming Cabinet members, however,
usually do not need to rely on a slobbering St. Bernard.
Traditionally, they are allowed bring along a couple of trusted
aides, just to have someone they can count on to look out for
their interests and not just the president's.

Buzz about town is that new Commerce Secretary Carlos M.
Gutierrez, former head of the Kellogg Co. in Battle Creek,
Mich., asked his longtime vice president of government affairs,
George Franklin, to be his senior adviser, apparently the only
non-administration aide Gutierrez wanted. Franklin, one of the
state's premier business lobbyists, who worked smoothly with
both sides of the aisle, did not want to come to Washington,
we're told. He preferred staying in Michigan and was looking
forward to retiring after many years at the cereal maker. But
Gutierrez insisted and Franklin finally consented.

Things were all set. Franklin was ready to go, even getting
ready to rent a townhouse in this area. But not so fast.

Seems the White House, presumably counselor Karl Rove, had heard
from Michigan Republicans who opposed Franklin. Word is it fell
to White House Chief of Staff Andrew H. Card Jr. to give
Gutierrez the news.

Unclear who opposed him or why, because Franklin's enemies are
said to be few and far between. But it may have to do with his
strong support of former Battle Creek mayor and freshman Rep.
John J.H. "Joe" Schwarz (R-Mich.) in his congressional race.
Schwarz, it turns out, was head of Sen. John McCain's 2000
presidential campaign in Michigan, where McCain won the GOP
primary, a painfully embarrassing blow to the Bush folks.
Whatever the reasons, Franklin is not coming to town.

So let's have a hearty Loop welcome for Gutierrez. This ain't
Battle Creek. Perhaps he'd like a *bichon frisé*?

The real reason was what I call the "Fox News bubble," which means only listening to those who are preaching your preferred version of the world. (The Democrats are just as guilty, so for the sake of parity we will call their version the CNBC bubble). God forbid alternative views are heard. Only true believers in the Republican Party are allowed in the cocoon. As one senior Democrat Senator told me after this episode, "If you're not willing to drink the Kool Aid, they don't want you." Suffice it to say, I was not that thirsty. I had retired from Kellogg to pursue the opportunity with Carlos and, after the "firing," Kellogg offered my job back to me. For this, I was grateful, but I'd gone too far down the road to turn back. It was time for me to move on, which I did with no regret and I have never looked back. My Kellogg career ended June 2005, but the final closure on this chapter of my life in fact occurred years later.

December 11, 2011, was a nondescript winter day in Atlanta, sunny and cool. My wife Molly, the very Republican woman I had been dating during Carlos' confirmation days, dropped me off at the airport for my flight to Michigan. As I walked up to my departure gate, I noticed Karl Rove typing away on his laptop. I thought to myself, "Now wouldn't that be something if he sat next to me on the plane." I took my seat in 3A and sure enough he sat down in 3B. Neither of us said anything for a few minutes, but as we stowed our belongings for takeoff, I turned to him and asked, "Aren't you Karl Rove?" to which he said, "Yes." I replied, "I'm George Franklin and I used to work for Carlos Gutierrez." He then launched into perfunctory exclamations extolling

Carlos' virtues. After a minute or so, I said to him, "Let me preface my comments by assuring you this is not an issue, you actually did me a favor, but remember the one guy Carlos wanted to take with him to Washington and you fired him before he was hired? That was me." The look on his face was priceless. After a few seconds he commented, "Didn't you support Kerry or something like that?" which I affirmed, but told him it was Engler who had come to object and that is why he vetoed me taking this position. He was speechless for a moment. Finally, he said, "Well, are you still working for Kellogg?" "No, they asked me if I wanted to come back, but I decided to start my own business using the publicity you helped me generate." I'm sure he was thinking that this would be a long, uncomfortable trip, but I never took anything he did personally and wasn't going to hold anything against him now. I was simply a casualty of typical, petty D.C. politics. So, on that plane, I took the high road, changed the subject and asked if he knew my wife, Molly Dye, who had been Chief of Staff to Georgia Senator Paul Coverdell. Rove broke into a smile and said, "You're married to Molly? How is she? I was talking to the Bushes the other day about Coverdell." Any sort of possible tension was averted. I always hate it when people hold you captive with conversation on a plane, so I went back to my book and he went back to his laptop. Upon landing, as we gathered our stuff, I inquired what brought him to Grand Rapids, Michigan and we small-talked a little bit about the Senate race. As we got ready to depart I remarked, "Well, I was going to wish you good luck, but since we're probably on opposite teams, how about just take care?" He grinned, "That's fair."

"Spending on contracts and lobbying propels a wave of new wealth in D.C. At the same time, big companies realized that a few million spent shaping legislation could produce windfall profits. They nearly doubled the cash they poured into the capital."

The Washington Post article on the new wave of wealth in D.C. in the last decade.

November 18, 2013

Chapter 12

The reason behind the sheer the number of lobbyists and the dollars spent lobbying is because it works. This startling revelation is akin to the recognition of gambling underway in Rick's Café in the movie Casablanca: They are both unspoken, but obvious.

Numerous studies have shown that lobbying is a very good investment, "comparable to the returns of the most blistering hedge fund," as *The Washington Post* put it in October 2011, "Hiring a top-flight lobbyist looks like a spectacular investment" and interest groups have taken heed of this revelation. The estimated number of lobbyists in D.C fluctuates wildly, anywhere from 12,000 to 17,000, depending on whose definition is used. The number of "real" lobbyists, those genuinely ingrained in the process and making an impact, is considerably less than the reported figures. Real lobbyists may or may not be registered, may or may not live in D.C. or its environs and may or may not be recognized as part of the government relations function. CEOs, movie stars, sports figures and the Senator's "old high school buddy" may be effective lobbyists, yet none would fall under the common definition.

Lobbying has taken place since there have been societies and organizations with disparate interest groups. The Medici family in Italy, cardinals vying to become Pope and even the gentlemen standing outside of the House of Commons in the famous painting by Liborio Prosperi in 1886 were all lobbyists. Any sizable group has interests within it. James Madison recognized this in the Federalist Papers when he referred to "factions" (i.e. interest groups) competing with each other.

"Special" in special interest is the pejorative used when a group disagrees with you. This is not unlike how a legal case is "leading" to lawyers when it supports his/her position. Mothers Against Drunk Driving (MADD), the National Restaurant Association (NRA), Sierra Club, Exxon, Future Farmers of America (FFA) and People For Ethical Treatment of Animals (PETA) are all special interest groups who need to advocate on behalf of their organizations against often-competing entities or government policies. They advocate using factual expertise along with political and financial pressure. The recipients of this advocacy tend to be individuals who are seeking higher office or re-election and in need of financial support.

Facts, constituents and fundraising are the three core components of lobbying. Constituent pressure and fundraising are the most commonly discussed and widely understood. The facts behind your policy position, however, are arguably the most important. One possible explanation as to why this aspect is not as well-recognized is because acknowledging the factual side of lobbying debunks the myth surrounding lobbying and, by extension, government: we all skeptically believe the whole system is always about politics and never "what is right."

Sure, there are instances where politics do prevail, but the day-to-day policy debates are fact-based. Trade associations, think tanks, corporations and consumer groups duel with data. I remember a time when conservatives found themselves outgunned by their opponents on the left, who were armed with the research and resources of the Brookings Institute, Urban Institute and other left-leaning think tanks. The rise of competing institutes, such as the Heritage Foundation and Hoover Institute on the right, are due to the critical nature of facts in the outcome of government debate.

Getting these crucial facts to the right place in government, be it Congress, an agency, or the White House, is what lobbyists do. Gary Pilnick, the General Counsel of Kellogg, astutely observed that lobbyists are, in essence, facilitators. I agree with this insight, but take it one step further; we are facilitators and also translators.

The lobbying process is generally straightforward and routine. We discern an issue developing in government, often through networking on the fundraising circuit or by way of trade associations, or sometimes it is brought to our attention by an affected department within our company. The lobbyist then taps into the company expertise to develop a "one-pager" (lobbyist lingo for executive summary), and this summary defines and translates the issue from corporate speak into government jargon.

One-pager in hand, the lobbyist acts as the company sherpa, identifying to where and whom resources from the company should go. You manage the whole process from identification, to translation to facilitation. If it is an issue before the Ways and Means Committee, you will probably need experts from your Tax Department. Matters concerning the Federal Trade Commission (FTC), you better call on Marketing or Legal. Issues before the Energy and Commerce Committee, FDA or USDA, may require Nutrition, Purchasing, Sales, etc. The lobbyist coaches the chosen participants, directs them and follows up in the process. The lobbyist also translates for the company what issues and problems are real and what are not. Coming back from D.C. on the company plane with a group of Kellogg executives, I recall hearing a corporate officer describe his "successful meeting" with a "concerned" Senator. I had to disabuse him of his misconception: "concern" means nothing, only action matters.

Through all of the facilitating and translating, lobbyists guide companies through the labyrinth of government utilizing political insight and their knowledge of the workings of the process. They also need a reservoir of earned and built-up trust and credibility. These are two attributes not normally associated with lobbyists, but they are fundamentally critical to the role they play. Members of Congress, State Legislators, and agency officials depend on lobbyists to give them the straight skinny on the merits of an issue as well as the politics surrounding it. If a lobbyist misleads or deceives, he/she will be out of business in short order. The system functions and relies on trust.

Interestingly, lobbyists and journalists are the only two private sector jobs protected by the Constitution. A provision in the First Amendment, with origins dating back to the Magna Carta in 1215, protects the right of the people "to petition the government for a redress of grievances." Lewis and Clark's expedition, the building of the Erie Canal and the Transcontinental Railroad, the man landing on the moon, as well as genetic research into a cure for cancer all occurred in part because of lobbying. Likewise, less exemplary happenings in history such as the Jack Abramhoff earmarks, the Teapot Dome scandal, Checkers and Koreagate transpired because of this profession. Lobbying, in all of its positive and negative glory, is an integral part of our system of government and will continue to be so long as there are competing interests and a Constitution.

[R] *indicates registered trademarks of Kellogg Company, except for Cheerios[R], which is a registered trademark of General Mills.*

Epilogue

Government Relations Fundamentals:

There is no form book on lobbying and corporate government relations. Each company, issue and overall situation will require different approaches. There are, however, some aspects which I believe my colleagues would agree are fundamental.

- Be politically realistic. Tempering the company's wish list to what is attainable as a practical matter is part of the government relations function. It often requires telling the emperor he has no clothes.

- Never ask a Member of Congress to do what is politically untenable. A Senator from Louisiana is not going to vote against the sugar industry, just like a Member from California is not going to oppose wine growers or Representatives from Michigan work against the auto manufacturers, regardless of how righteous you think your cause may be.

- Make your "ask" as concise and specific as possible and explain how it will benefit the constituents of that Member.

- Demonstrate how the request will help the affected agency or department accomplish THEIR objectives. In other words, how it will further the mission of the entity.

- During meetings, be prepared to discuss the benefits and the drawbacks of the proposal, both substantively and politically. Be up front about which groups, organizations and companies are friend and foe.

- In every meeting, ask them to do something, such as write a letter or call another Member. Expressions of concern and interest are of little practical value, unless accompanied by action.

- Leave behind a "one-pager" or some kind of synopsis with relevant background information. In essence, do their homework.

- Finally, make yourself or other members of your group available for questions, concerns or any further information and then periodically follow-up with the staff or the Member to make sure your request(s) are being fulfilled and that they have everything they need.

Seeking Economic Incentives:

Securing economic incentives requires the same case-by-case approach as other lobbying efforts. Each situation will vary according to the company, the location and the scope of the project. There are, however, some fundamentals which apply almost universally.

- Economic development officials, in and out of government, can be trusted to keep information confidential. It is the lifeblood of their profession and never once in my experience was this breached.

- Incentives are either statutory or discretionary with negotiations lying at the heart of the process.

- Be forthcoming with the company's plans and objectives. It is easier to address difficult issues at the beginning of the discussions then have them arise as a surprise as you are trying to finalize an agreement.

- Avoid corporate arrogance. Treat the local and state officials as professionals who are doing a job and entitled to being treated in a responsive, courteous manner.

- Be mindful and respectful of local political, tax and economic constraints.

- Within your company be prepared to draw on an array of disciplines. Everything from Legal, Tax, Human Resources, Public Affairs and Supply Chain departments will be called upon and will be needed to participate in a timely fashion in order to meet the company's timeline. Prepping them in advance will help you and them to meet that objective.

- Finally, make sure the company and the relevant departments understand the granting of incentives is not a "one and done" deal. There will be responsibilities which accompany the grant and extend through the life of the incentive which will require resources to comply. Reports will need to be filed, audits will be conducted and periodic updates, meetings and community responsibilities will ensue.